Pagan Portals

Planetary Magic

A friendly introduction to creating modern
magic with the seven energies

Pagan Portals
Planetary Magic

A friendly introduction to creating modern
magic with the seven energies

Rebecca Beattie

MOON
BOOKS
Winchester, UK
Washington, USA

JOHN HUNT PUBLISHING

First published by Moon Books, 2023
Moon Books is an imprint of John Hunt Publishing Ltd., No. 3 East Street, Alresford
Hampshire SO24 9EE, UK
office@jhpbooks.net
www.johnhuntpublishing.com
www.moon-books.net

For distributor details and how to order please visit the 'Ordering' section on our website.

ISBN: 978 1 80341 176 7
978 1 80341 177 4 (ebook)
Library of Congress Control Number: 2022934447

A CIP catalogue record for this book is available from the British Library.

Design: Matthew Greenfield

UK: Printed and bound by CPI Group (UK) Ltd, Croydon, CR0 4YY
Printed in North America by CPI GPS partners

We operate a distinctive and ethical publishing philosophy in
all areas of our business, from our global network of authors to
production and worldwide distribution.

Contents

Also by Rebecca Beattie

Nature Mystics: The Literary Gateway to Modern Paganism
978-1-78279-799-9

This book is dedicated to my Witchlets – those who joined me each month at the Young Urban Witch classes at Treadwell's Books in Bloomsbury, London, aka Witch Club. I am intensely proud of all of you and the lives you are continuing to build. I learned so many things in your company.

Foreword

Sometime around the turn of the Millennium, I decided to take a year off from my chosen career (acting) to spend time developing a spiritual life. I had no idea but, at the end of my twenties, I had reached what we refer to in witch-circles as your 'Saturn-return'. Having spent your younger years striving to get to where you think you should be, you discover the world is not quite what you imagined it would be. In your astrological chart, the planet Saturn comes back round to the place it was at the moment of your birth, and you start questioning everything. Common questions can include, 'why am I here?', 'what is my purpose in life?' and, most frighteningly, 'surely there must be more to life than this?'

I was lucky. I grew up in the middle of Dartmoor, one of England's national parks, and was surrounded by nature. Nature was everything for me – my inspiration, my nurturer, my confidante. However, certain that excitement (and my acting career) was to be found somewhere else, I had been determined to leave at the earliest opportunity and strike out in my chosen field. As most young people find, when they get to the place they were striving to reach, it is never quite what you thought it was. I was in London, and, several years into discovering my pagan path, I realised I had become cut off from nature, and needed to reconnect. It was then that I stumbled across an internet post. Treadwell's Books, an Occult bookshop in central London was running a course for solitary witches. I signed up, and went along, slightly terrified at what I would discover, however, I needn't have worried. Treadwell's was to become my home from home. It is an independent bookshop, established by Christina Oakley Harrington, and has (against all odds) thrived in a climate of online shopping, a place and time where even the larger chain-shops have been traded out of existence. Treadwell's is different. It is a bookshop staffed by the most highly educated and gifted people you may stumble across in London, and it is also a community centre, which draws in pagans of all types and ages from across the globe. It was there that I learned all about Pre-Modern Planetary Magic for the first time.

Fast forward nearly twenty years, having gone through Wiccan training and joined a coven, I had a seed of an idea in my head to teach a self-care workshop for worn out witches. I had started to co-present a workshop on self-care for frontline drug workers in my day-job and thought that this would translate really well into a short workshop for community elders too. I approached Christina at Treadwell's. When I presented my idea to Christina, her response was 'Sure, but have you thought about...'

Christina's idea was far more exciting.

'Young creatives are crying out for a teacher', she told me. 'And that teacher may well be you'. At the time, I had spent the last three years studying part time for my PhD, and I had been too afraid to teach or think of myself as becoming a teacher. But as is often the way, when the idea of something seems too immense to handle, you have to break it down into bite sized pieces. Becoming a teacher might be daunting but taking on a workshop or two for young creative folk didn't feel as scary, and so the idea of the Young Urban Witches, or Witchlets was born. The next thing I knew, just when I thought I was calling in at the shop to check on how my necklaces were selling, or to drop off a few volumes of my first book, *Nature Mystics*, I would be introduced to a young person or two, who was excitedly looking forward to attending their first workshop.

Over the course of 2017, the Witchlets were to be the making of me. The class started out small – just eight or nine witchlets. They were mostly women, LGBTQIA or non-binary folk, and mostly under the age of thirty. They were people drawn to the archetype of the Witch – all immensely creative, neuro-diverse, and all looking for a 'safe' space to meet and connect, without the fashion for being aloof and uncaring. We created a space where they could explore the idea of witchcraft, learn about the practicalities of planetary magic, connect their spiritual lives to a community and their creative practices, and ask questions whenever they arose. It was part magical training, part creative exploration, and part support group.

I began with a course of seven workshops, one a month, on practical planetary magic. Each workshop looked at each planetary power, its symbols and sigils, its cousins, and counterparts across other pantheons of the world, and then moved on to an element of practical magic – the crafting element of the witchcraft. We played with making incense, making bath salts, making amulets or magical herbal pouches – I say 'played' as that is the best way to approach creative explorations. When the COVID pandemic began in 2019, the classes moved online to Zoom, and continued. By now they were bringing in students from across the globe, and of all ages.

This is the book that has grown out of those workshops. Christina and the Witchlets turned me into a teacher... and for that I will be eternally grateful. I now invite you to explore the ideas in these pages and discover Planetary Magic for yourselves.

Introduction

The Modern Witch's Path

You take the path that leads you through the ancient woodland, with a sense of wonder at the abundance of nature around you. Sunlight shimmers on the leaves that dance in the breeze: oaks, stand cheek by jowl with beeches, wild apple trees and tall, sombre larches. It is a warm day, even in the shadows of the great green guardians of this space, and the birds are singing loudly from the branches. You carry a basket as you go, gathering wild herbs that grow at the feet of the trees, and there is no sense of hurry in your step. As the path turns to the left, you catch a faint smell of wood-smoke on the breeze, and you realise you are nearly there. It won't be long before you arrive.

Squirrels undulate across the branches above your head, causing the leaves to rustle and the odd acorn to fall and land at your feet; you spot a deer, running away in fright once it is alerted to your presence; crows call out to each other. Then, turning again on the path, you arrive at a clearing in the forest, and the cottage is in front of you. Its low thatched roof is well camouflaged with the forest behind it; the garden at the front of it is busy with a plethora of herbs, and flowers. A vegetable patch is just visible on the right-hand side. Approaching the front door, you spy a yellow-eyed black cat watching you from the window, and as you knock at the door, the cat jumps down into the dark room behind. The door slowly opens, and the witch stands there in front of you.

Is she old or is she young? You can hardly tell. Are you the visitor or are you the witch? All you know is that your arrival has been anticipated. As you cross the threshold and enter the house, your fears are left behind.

Your eyes gradually adjust to the dim light inside. A warm

4

fire burns in the grate, and a cauldron hangs over the hearth, emitting wisps of steam. A wooden dresser to the left of the fireplace is lined with glass jars with all manner of herbs and strange looking substances. You read several of the labels in wonder. Frankincense Tears, dandelion root, amaranth blossoms, sandalwood chips. At the centre of the kitchen is an old oak table, its surface worn smooth with age, and littered with books: some of them are written in strange symbols, and others are hidden under piles of parchment and quills. The cat that was in the window before, now sits in a rocking chair by the hearth, regarding you with watchful eyes. You could almost imagine the human-like intelligence that resides behind those eyes. Your turn with your wide-eyed gaze and begin to find the words to ask for what you need.

That's how witches live, right? A cross between Terry Pratchett's Granny Weatherwax, and Mary Webb's Mister Beguildy, they live in the woods. They are nearly always colourful in their dress, and eccentric in their behaviour. They are outsiders, half feral, and slightly disturbing. We are the edge-walkers, the people that inhabit the liminal spaces, after all. But there is also another archetype that has been growing in recent years – that of the Love Witch – sleeping her way through the town and burying the men she has become bored with. Or the glamorous charmed witches, destroying demons whilst looking for love, supporting each other in their sisterhood. Or the Sabrina-esque witch, wide-eyed and part of a Satanic cult.

The reality of most witches is quite different from the archetypes we imagine. While each generation may come to this path by the romance of the *Priestess of Avalon*, or tales of Herne the Hunter, the younger generations coming in will be different again. Intensely creative, the younger generation of witches do not ride in wearing crushed velvet and tie dye, they are far too stylish for that. They may be brought by the aesthetic qualities of #witchesofinstagram, and by the need to find a new way of surviving in this online digital age, where everything including your underwear is plastered over social media.

Many of us live in urban settings, due to economic necessity or familial ties, and our homes are more likely to be set amidst a backdrop of urban noise – sirens, traffic, the neighbour's loud music – than the sound of squirrels and birdsong. Modern life is not the perfect picture dreamed up in so many fictional settings. Some of us are lucky enough to be able to live in more rural settings, closer to nature, but not all.

So, what on earth is a Witch to do when they need to do a spell working to bring love into their life, or to help themself along with some intensive self-care? Go and gather wild roses in the woodlands, skipping along the path with a handwoven wicker basket? Or pop down to the local international supermarket on the corner, and buy a bag of rose petal tea? That's not to say the hand-woven wicker basket isn't intensely alluring, and a beautiful option if you can get it. We often have deeply unrealistic expectations of what our lives should be like, and then waste far too much energy cracking ourselves over the head with the 'bad-witch' stick when we don't live up to them. As my best friend is so fond of telling me, 'Stop should-ing all over yourself, it's a very dirty habit'.

The need for perfection will stop you in your tracks and prevent you from achieving anything. Instead of aspiring to something unobtainable and then failing miserably, this is the modern witch's guide to working creatively with the seven archetypal energies that swirl and envelop this planet Earth that we live on, known otherwise as pre-modern planetary magic. Or if you prefer, this is the crap witch's guide to imperfect but effective twenty-first century witch crafting, using traditional folk magic and its energetic correspondences as a framework.

Chapter 1

Magical Problems and Planetary Solutions

Before I even start laying the groundwork on what each planetary energy is, and what their qualities are, before I even start suggesting what magic is and how you can make your spell craft more effective, I thought it might be helpful to jump right in with a list of magical aims, and which planetary energy you might want to work with. You can then go straight to the chapter on that planet to read about it in more depth, as well as have a look at the suggestions I have made for different spell workings under each one.

Here then is an alphabetical list of intentions, and which planet you need to work with. This is not exhaustive, and you will discover your own as you continue your journey with the seven energies...

Abundance – Jupiter
Anger (dispelling) – Venus
Animal communication – Mercury
Animal, return home – Venus
Animal, Protection from attack – Mars
Animal well-being – Sun
Anxiety – Sun
Athletics, speed – Mars, Mercury
Athletics, endurance – Sun
Astral travel – Moon, Mercury
Attractiveness -Venus
Authority, to gain – Jupiter
Baby blessing – Moon, Jupiter
Betrayal – Saturn

Breaking contracts – Sutton
Business and Commerce- Mercury
Conflict (soothing) – Venus
Courage – Mars
Cursing (breaking) – Saturn
Death – Saturn
Grief – Moon
Desire – Mars, Venus
Depression (relieving) – Sun
Difficult conversations – Venus, Saturn
Divination – Moon
Doors (opening the way) – Mercury
Dreams – Moon
Enemies (making peace) – Venus
Evil eye (protection from) – Mars, Saturn
Fame and renown – Sun
Fertility – Moon
Financial success – Jupiter (for long-lasting), Mercury (for fast)
Friendship (attracting) – Sun, Venus
Gossip (stopping) – Mars, Saturn
Good luck – Mercury, Sun
Happiness – Sun
Heartbreak (healing) – Venus
Healing – Sun
Health – Sun
Love (Attracting) – Venus
Love (keeping) – Venus, Jupiter
Love (inspiring passion) – Venus, Mars
Ending – Venus, Saturn
Lust – Mars
Magic – Moon
Marriage – Venus
Medical professionals – Mercury, Sun

Mental powers – Mercury

Masculinity – Mars

Money, wealth – Jupiter, Mercury, Sun

Negotiation – Jupiter

Nightmares – Sun

Oath breaking – Saturn

Passion – Mars, Venus

Patronage – Jupiter

Peace – Venus

Persuasion – Jupiter, Mercury

Popularity – Sun

Protection – Saturn, Mars

Purification – Sun, Moon, Mercury, Mars, Saturn

Resilience – Sun

Restraint – Saturn, Sun

Risk-taking – Mercury

Seafaring protection – Venus

Sex – Mars

Sleep – Moon

Spirituality – Moon

Study – Mercury, Jupiter

Success – Sun

Tarot (see divination)

Theft (prevention) Saturn

Travel – Mercury

Wealth – Jupiter

Wisdom – Jupiter

Worry (calming) – Venus, Sun, Jupiter

To help you get more of an overview of the seven energetic powers, I have included a table that gives a summary of the main headlines for each planet.

	Moon	Mercury	Venus	Sun	Mars	Jupiter	Saturn
	Monday	Wednesday	Friday	Sunday	Tuesday	Thursday	Saturday
	Silver	Orange	Pink or green	Gold or yellow	Red	Purple or blue	Black
	9	8	7	6	5	4	3
	Women's Mysteries Fertility Clairvoyance Divination, Cyclical events, dreaming.	Communication, travel, intellect, learning, computers, fast acting, mutable energy, stock market.	Love, self care, physical comfort, luxury, love, love and more love, reconciliation and romance.	Success, health, youth, Health, healing, protection, physical energy, fulfilment.	War, assertiveness, boundary setting, bold and not to be argued with.	Harmony, law, expansion and enlargement, ownership, wealth and fortune, music.	Grounding, home, life, steadiness, self, banishing, slow moving and heavy.
	poppy, evening primrose, iris, mandrake, mugwort, jasmine, sandalwood, lemon balm, dandelion (in its seed phase).	Lavender, bergamot, dill, fennel, lemon herbs, mint, papyrus, parsley.	Rose, hibiscus, geranium, iris, heather, larkspur, lilac, magnolia, willow, mallow, myrtle.	Marigold, bay, saffron, benzoin, cedar, frankincense, sandalwood, chamomile, orange, dandelion (in its flower phase)	Gorse, thistles, tobacco, garlic, wormwood, nettle, ginger, hawthorn, dragon's blood, Chilli, basil, cumin, coriander.	Basil, violet, oak, barley, wheat, borage, star anise, honeysuckle, betony, dock, horse chestnut.	Patchouli, sulphur, tamarind, amaranth, belladonna, ivy, hemlock, henbane, yew, wolfsbane.

Chapter 2

Working with the Seven Energetic Powers of Planetary Magic

Before we go any further, it's important to set a little groundwork, as this is essential in understanding why we are here. Even if you are an experienced magical practitioner, I would recommend you read this through, as it helps set the scene for the rest of the book. You may disagree, and that is fine, I am not in the business of telling you what to believe. This is merely a sharing of my model of the world. We all have one, and it is unique to each of us.

In this section I have laid out a few paragraphs that introduce some of the background principles to working with planetary magic.

Working Non-Binary Magic

While you might be thinking that planets sound like a celestial thing, and what's that got to do with working magic on Earth, I consider the seven 'planetary' powers to be earthly energies that swirl and flow all around us. In the worldview of our magical ancestors, everything on Earth was ruled by one of the seven energies that flow through plants, stones, personalities, body parts, activities, animals, places, numbers, and a host of other aspects of earthly life. Looking up at the Heavens, they reasoned that each of these energies must be ruled by a planetary body, and eventually they went through the process of naming them after their gods. In different cultures they were ascribed to different deities, and the final one that stuck was the Roman pantheon. However, the planets are not the same as the deities they were named for, and if you find the Roman pantheon off-

11

putting, you could equally work with different deity-names and still get the same results. Therefore, if Saturn feels patriarchal, work with Binah instead. Or if Mars is too much, then Sekhmet carries similar energy. It's the quality of the planetary energy that is important, not the name, and while the deities they were named for might be ascribed masculine or feminine genders, the planetary energies aren't gendered in this book as I don't consider them to be gendered. We often ascribe gender as a way of drawing us close to an energy and understanding it in human terms, but that can also be off-putting. If you want to work in a non-binary way, check the section of each chapter on cousins and counterparts, where I have suggested alternative deities / archetypes you might prefer to work with.

Magic, Kaballah, and other terminology...

You may come across variations in the spelling of certain key words – magic or magick, Kaballah or Qabala or Kaballa... They all come down to personal preference. The word 'occult' often gives people who are unfamiliar to this field a reason to give an involuntary shudder. It doesn't mean we are practicing devil worship (and don't get me started on that one as we could write a whole Pagan Portal of its own on why Pagan witchcraft isn't devil worship). It just means we are in the realms of mystical or magical belief. Other terms will appear throughout the text, but as I use them, I will explain what they mean.

What Magic(k) is

The key is also in understanding what magic is. Magick, in the context of Aleister Crowley's Thelema, is a term used to show and differentiate the occult from performance magic and is defined as "the Science and Art of causing Change to occur in conformity with Will", including both "mundane" acts of will as well as ritual magic. What often gets forgotten when people repeat that quote, is that Crowley also wrote a second part to it – "it is theoretically possible to cause in any object any change of which that object is capable by nature"[1]. Just like business-world SMART goals, the outcome will only work if it is realistic and attainable in the first place. You can't force something to become something it was never meant to be. The universe has an uncanny way of not answering your prayer when it was never meant to be yours in the first place. I could be the most excellent practitioner of magic in the world today, but any attempts I make at turning myself into the Queen of the Faeries will be met with astonished silence.

Just a note on scepticism – I am one of the most sceptical people I know, and there is always a little part of me that stands some way off thinking that none of this can be possible. Of course, this is just one model of the world, and you don't have to believe any of it if you don't want to. I approach my magic like I do the rest of my life – I am happier in the world when I allow myself freedom in playing with my creativity, and my spiritual and creative lives are inextricably linked – I cannot have one without the other. You may choose to see this as a book to help you connect with your creativity, it might be there to help you to explore the archetype of the Witch a little further. To get results by any magical system, you need pop your logical brain on pause, and give yourself permission to allow the possibility of what might happen. If you can't do that, then act as if you believe it might be possible.

In this book, I mostly refer to magic with a 'c', but I am not talking about stagecraft, I am talking about occult practices.

Scott Cunningham, a magical practitioner of the late Twentieth Century who wrote many fabulous books about natural magic, wrote that for magic to work, the person needed three things: the need for the magic to work (not to be confused with a desire), an appropriate emotional response, and the knowledge of magical lore. Therefore, it is important to not just rely on working intuitively, in Cunningham's view.[2]

Why a system of magic (and therefore training) can be important

Working with magic is a bit like working with Tarot cards. You can learn the meaning of each individual card, but unless you have a structure to place the cards into, they make very little sense on their own and lose a crucial layer of meaning. While I am part of an initiatory witchcraft tradition (and part of a coven) I also have a solitary practice which is grounded in hedge witchcraft – I work with herbs, essential oils, and nature-based materials. When working with plants, herbs, oils, talismans, and sigils, you can understand each one individually, but that is a long way round the business of learning magic. If you have a system of correspondences to place them in, they start to form a much bigger picture. The system of seven pre-modern planetary powers is the one I learned when I was in coven training, and it is the system my teacher was taught, and her teacher was taught. If we trace our lines of concordance back through history, it was the also the magical system used in both high and low magical traditions. What do I mean by High and Low magic?

A Potted History of Western Magic: High Magic and Low Magic

Most scholars agree that Modern Pagan Witchcraft (which many witches practice today) emerged publicly following the repeal of the Witchcraft Act in the British Isles in 1951. It doesn't mean witchcraft didn't exist before, but the pagan version didn't. As much as we would love to believe that there is evidence of a pagan practice stretching back through an unbroken link to the Pre-Christian era, there is scant evidence of that line being unbroken by a millennium and a half of a dominant Christian world view. One reason for this is that in the Pre-Christian eras, most systems of learning were passed through oral traditions, and not written down. We can find archaeological evidence of pre-Christian beliefs – through excavations of sites such as Stonehenge, Whitehorse Hill on Dartmoor, and others we know what was done, but we have no idea why.

Witchcraft has existed throughout human history, but not all witches are pagan, both throughout history and now. A cursory exploration of historical folk charms will reveal that the words that many of the charms rely on to work are monotheistic in feel – they very often invoke magic in the name of the Father, the Son and the Holy Ghost. (Threes are always common in magic). While many of us would love to imagine a *Mists of Avalon* style beginning to this belief system, the closest link to that is through the popular fiction that drew many of us to this path in the first place. There were early covens that existed before 1951, but scholars lean towards their practicing a largely ceremonial tradition, rather than a pagan one.

Despite this, most scholars also agree that the origins of the Magic practiced by Pagan Witches today was rooted in two main traditions – High Magic (the ceremonial magic practiced by groups such as the Hermetic Order of the Golden Dawn in the Victorian period, the Rosicrucians, the Freemasons etc) and the Low Magic traditions of Cunning Folk. Cunning folk were the traditional charmers that were often found on the outskirts of communities – these were the people you would turn to for help if you thought your neighbour had cursed you and caused your cows to stop giving milk, or if you wanted to attract that lover who just could not see you despite all your yearning. Cunning folk often wore outlandish dress – they set themselves apart from the rest of the community by being that slightly odd person that lived on their own in the woods, they were very often male (although cunning women did exist), and they were always literate, another unusual trait for the time, and one that was crucial for how they learned their craft. Cunning folk knew how to work with herbs to heal, as well as charms to bring magical results to fruition. Most of their work (ironically) was in creating charms to guard against witchcraft, which at that time was thought to be maleficium – a harmful form of cursing. To learn more about these, I would recommend the work of Professor Ronald Hutton, or Professor Owen Davies (both in the References section at the back).

What both groups of practitioners (Low Magic and High Magic) have in common is that they both studied the same books of learning, which happen to be the same books that Modern Pagan Witches read now as part of their coven training. Traditional pre-modern grimoires like Cornelius Agrippa's *Three Books of Occult Philosophy*, or the *Key of Solomon*, or *The Picatrix*. If you browse the shelves in any occult bookstore, you will still find copies of these books.

Over time, the cunning folk began to fade away, although reports of them often circulated in different areas in the latter part of the Twentieth Century, just as Modern Pagan Witchcraft was beginning to emerge into popular culture. Obviously, groups such as Freemasons still exist, and all these groups had an influence on how Modern Paganism developed in the Twentieth Century. If you are reading this book somewhere other than the British Isles and are wondering why this history is so Britain-centric, that's because I am writing from a Wiccan perspective – the branch of Modern Pagan Witchcraft that emerged from the UK in Gerald Gardner's work following the repeal of that pesky Witchcraft Act.

The clue for why this little potted history is important in understanding planetary magic is in the casual mention of Grimoires...

Grimoires and the Seven Planetary Powers

The Seven Planetary Powers are recorded in the Grimoire tradition, but this system of magic is even older than that. It dates to ancient times, long before many of the Grimoires we refer to now were even written down (the history of our own written system of communication begins much later than the history of humankind). Back as far as Ancient Babylon (2nd Millennium BCE), humans were observing the movement of the seven planetary powers across their night skies, although they did not have the powerful telescopes we have now, so what they could see was limited. According to D'Este and Rankine in their book of *Practical Planetary Magick*, in Ancient Babylon the planets were referred to as the 'Wandering Stars'. While the constellations stayed together in formation whilst moving across the sky, the planets were celestial bodies that would be observed to appear in different places over time.[3]

The Ancient Egyptians continued this observation, and they also began to attribute their own deities with the celestial bodies, as did the Ancient Greeks, but the names of the even planets as we know them today are taken from their renaming after the Roman pantheon. All of this took place at a point in our history before Galileo (1564-1642) observed that the planets revolve around the sun. To the ancient astrologers, we lived in an Earth-centric universe. This was not the flat-earth theory – they understood we live on a spherical world, but they believed Earth was at the centre of the universe, and everything else revolved around it. When we look at the world view presented by this system of magic, it is therefore very different from our contemporary view of science and the universe.

In the Pre-modern Universe, there are only seven planets revolving around Earth – Moon, Mercury, Venus, Mars, Sun, Jupiter, and Saturn. It was believed that each of these planetary powers shone its rays down on the earth, and certain elements in nature which were more pre-disposed to soaking up the rays of each planet, would take on its qualities. This means there are plants, stones, foods, animals, places, vocations, and parts of the human body that are all under the dominion of one of the planetary powers. These were later listed by astrologers and authors, such as Cornelius Agrippa (1486-1535). Agrippa was a German polymath – he studied medicine, law, he was a soldier, a theologian, and an astrologer, and he wrote one of the most widely referenced Grimoires we have on our bookshelves. He wasn't the first to discover planetary magic, but his Grimoire, *The Three Books of Occult Philosophy*, is one of the earliest written records we have of that form of planetary magic that occult practitioners still use today.

Those of you who are astrologers may be wondering what's happened to Uranus and Neptune (I won't even bother to make my excuses for poor Pluto here). You will have noticed that they don't appear in the pre-Modern planetary line up. That's due to simple physics. In the Pre-Modern period, those planets couldn't be seen, so no one knew they existed. If you start questioning me about the qualities of Uranus and Neptune and what they can be used for, I will probably stare at you blankly, as less trained in Modern Astrology than I am in the pre-modern systems. I am aware they exist, and have a vague notion of their qualities, but this system of magic dismisses them entirely. In your own practice, you may choose to re-introduce them to the flock, but for now, let's concentrate on the other seven before they make a bid for freedom.

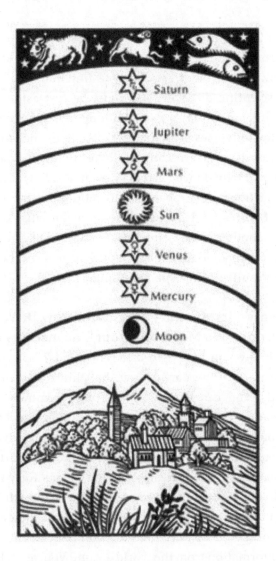

Where do the Elements Fit in?

The four or five elements and the Seven Planetary powers are all systems of correspondence. They allow us to ascribe meanings and properties to different stones, herbs, oils, animals, and places. If you are wondering where the elements fit with the planets, they were believed to have been earth-bound. The Earth consisted of things that were made of Earth, Air, Fire and Water.

If your 21ˢᵗ Century head feels as if it's about to burst with that information, and you can't quite put your modern head on pause... if your inner geek is protesting that seven hundred years of scientific discovery can't just be cast aside like that, then I invite you to play a game with me. Imagine that all that exists in the universes is all that is visible to the naked eye.

So, if this Pre-modern Universal world view is a hopelessly outdated one, why do we need to know it now? I would present two reasons (there are probably many more). One is the need for systems of correspondence to help you make sense of magical attributes, another is the Grimoires. For a third, it's also helpful to start thinking about *how* magic works, as this will help you to get better results in your spell working.

Twenty-First Century Magic and How It Works
Your Conscious Mind, and Your Unconscious Mind

Did you know you have two different minds? You have your conscious mind – the part of you that thinks and does logic, and words, and can handle seven (plus or minus two) bits of information at any one moment. And then you have your unconscious mind – the part that controls your body for you, moves your muscles when you want to move a part of your body, breathes for you, dreams for you, learns for you. If you tried to do that with your conscious mind, you wouldn't be able to do anything else. Your unconscious can handle the two billion bits of information that are fired at you every second – all that sensory information from the world around you, as well as what is happening within your own body. Psychologists used to call this the subconscious mind. I was taught to refer to it as the unconscious, because this is not subservient to your conscious mind – it is very much in control of your ship. The trick to working well with your unconscious is to ensure your conscious and unconscious minds are both in rapport with each other, but here's the thing – the unconscious mind doesn't understand lexical instructions all that well. It doesn't do language – that's a job for your conscious mind. The unconscious mind works in pictures and symbols. It likes colours and tastes, and pictures and stories. It is like a little seven-year-old child on your inside, and it also doesn't understand negative instructions, interpreting a 'don't do...' instruction into a 'do...' instead.

The unconscious mind also has a very clever method for filtering out things that it does not need and selecting the things that it wants to engage with. This is called the Reticular Activating System, or RAS. When you set your RAS to focus on blue butterflies, you may notice that you suddenly see blue butterflies everywhere you go. Or if you set your RAS to help you seek out a new job in a bank, its likely you will suddenly see adverts for jobs in banks everywhere you go. We are also going to borrow a term that you may have come across in the business world when working on goal-setting – SMART goals (Specific Measurable Achievable Realistic Timed). Whether you are goal setting in your working life, or doing spells in your magical life, or sending a prayer for something up to heaven (because all these things are aspects of the same process) SMART is a useful thing to know, as it helps you to frame things in a way that your unconscious mind can understand. Why all this talk about the unconscious? For the modern witch to work effectively with magic there is one other thing you need to understand about the unconscious mind – it is also the source of all the magic.

Magic isn't necessarily something that only comes from outside of you, bestowed on you by an external supernatural agency or deity, although you might prefer to believe it is. This is not to say that the divine doesn't have a role in it all (I think the truth is somewhere in between and the magic we make is a co-creation between us and the Universe, but I will leave you to make up your own mind). Whichever view you ascribe to, you do need to take an active role in working magic, and those SMART goals that you were taught to do at work each year during your annual appraisal, work equally as well when setting a spell goal as they do for setting an objective in your day job.

The other role your Unconscious mind plays is as a go-between – between your conscious mind and your higher self – i.e., that part of you that is Divine, or is part of the collective unconscious, as Carl Jung might have phrased it. While I view nature as the source of my contact with the Divine, and the work I do is an outer expression of that inner relationship, this can work equally well if you are an atheist, or a practitioner of any other spiritual belief. For me, the system of working with the seven planetary powers is really a way of communicating with your unconscious mind, which needs those colours and symbols and scents and metaphors to understand what you need it to do, when it doesn't communicate linguistically. Your conscious mind is there to imprint your will, to help you to state your intention, and the unconscious mind is there to make it happen. One without the other just won't work. I could have called this the SMART Witch's Guide to Planetary Goal Setting, but that just sounds like a coaching textbook, and not a book about magical techniques. But hopefully you will get where we are heading.

If you want to learn more about this, then I would sign-post you to the work of Carl Jung, or to the work of Richard Bandler and John Grinder who developed Neuro-Linguistic Programming (NLP), which is another one of my areas of training.

Working with Kabbalah

When we get to the actual planets themselves, you will notice that some of the correspondences I give you refer to archangels and something called Sephiroth, which can feel a little alien if you identify as pagan and don't normally work with angelic beings. These correspondences are taken from Kabbalah, a system of magic that we have inherited through our Hermetic Order of the Golden Dawn ancestry. But what is it?

Kabbalah is topic that really requires a whole Pagan Portal of its own, so it would be very difficult to do it justice in one short paragraph (I have listed some books in the bibliography that you might want to look out for if you wish to explore this area of working in more depth). Some witches spend a lifetime exploring it. Simply put, Ellen Cannon Reid writes that 'It has been called a framework, a stepladder for spiritual growth, and a tool for the study of comparative religion'[4]. Kabbalah (you will see many different spellings) is a system of working, both magically and spiritually. It originates in the work of the Jewish Mystics as a form of esoteric teachings created to explain the relationship between the divine and the universe. From the renaissance period onwards, Jewish Kabbalah texts were then obtained by people of non-Jewish cultures and studied. At this point in history, the Christianised version of the Kabbalah began, as well as the Hermetic Kabbalah, and the three branches began to develop along different traditions.

It is that third branch, the Hermetic tradition that witches still study today as part of their coven training. While Kabbalah is something people spend a lifetime studying, this is just a quick snapshot and can't do the system justice in such a short space of time. If you take one piece of information away, it is important to be aware of the Kabbalistic Tree of Life diagram – you will have seen it on your travels, no doubt. The Kabbalistic Tree of Life is a map of the spiritual life, designed to act as a guide on the journey from the earthly plane at Malkuth, to the realm of the divine, which sits above the crown at Kether. Each of the ten circles on that diagram is referred to as a 'Sephira' and represents an area of spiritual enlightenment that the kabbalistic practitioner is expected to study and master. Each of the sephiroth is then linked by a path, twenty-two in number (which you will notice is the same number as the Major Arcana in Tarot), which lead the practitioner onto the next sephira in their journey.

The reason this information is found in a book of planetary magic is that each of the sephiroth corresponds to one of the seven pre-modern planets, according to the practice developed by the Hermetic Order of the Golden Dawn. For those of you who are numerically minded, there are three left over – Malkuth (which corresponds to Earth), Chockmah (which is often associated with the zodiac) and Kether (which corresponds to the crown, or godhead). In modern astrological interpretations, you will see Chockmah being associated with Uranus, and Kether being associated with Neptune. That will give you a hint that it is a modern interpretation, and not the Hermetic version because, as we know, those planets did not exist in the pre-modern worldview. It is from the Kabbalistic Tree of Life that we get another layer of our planetary correspondences.

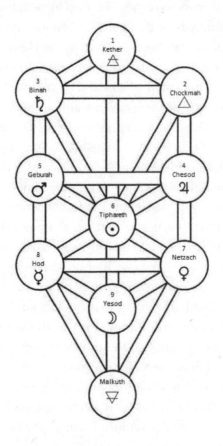

Sigil Magic and the Planetary Kameas

Cornelius Agrippa, whom we met when we were looking at Grimoires, also introduces something called the kamea for each planet. Kameas are magical number squares that can be used to develop sigils (a symbol considered to have magical power) which can be carved onto candles, written on parchment, or even, written on the body in oil or paint, if you want them to be. While we also have the alchemical or astrological glyphs (another kind of symbol) that we used to identify the planets, sigils are a form of shorthand that hold the power of the planet – it's a way of tapping into those powers and bringing their energy into your magical working.

Each planet has its own kamea which is based on its own planetary number. This means that the Moon has a kamea that is made up of a 9 x 9 square of numbers, whereas Jupiter's kamea is a 4 x 4 square. The numbers do more than just languish about in the squares. If you enjoy numerology, you are going to love this bit! You will notice that in any given direction in the Jupiterian kamea, the numbers all add up to 34.

4	14	15	1
9	7	6	12
5	11	10	8
16	2	3	13

Using the kamea for each planet, Agrippa then produced a sigil by drawing lines that touch on each number in the kamea, and express the qualities of the planet, which are referred to as planetary seals. Once we get into each planet in detail, I will list both the kamea and the seal of each planet. To really go into more depth on this topic, I would urge you to get hold of a copy of Agrippa for yourself – when researching a topic fully, it is always best to go straight to the original source and make Agrippa's acquaintance more fully.

When working with herbs – please use caution!

While the herbs under each planetary power are listed in its correspondence table, you may choose to work with an herb in its dried form, or as an essential oil. Please do exercise some caution with some of the herbs – while you may safely drink a pot of jasmine tea whilst celebrating the moon, some of the other herbs are not meant for consumption – particularly when we get to Saturn, who governs most of the stinky and poisonous herbs – so always ask the advice of your local herbalist before drinking and check the contraindications before use. Some herbs are especially to be avoided if you are pregnant.

There are many ways to work with herbs, and if this is an area of interest, you can explore the list of suggested reading in the appendices. It's also best to avoid buying herbs on well-known large websites from sellers you do not know. They may be cheap, and delivered straight to your door, but you also may find yourself with a highly toxic substance on your hands without the usual safeguards that a qualified herbalist will put in place.

Some herbs can be used in teas (when they are safe for consumption), they can be added to bath salts (when they are safe for application on the skin), they can be added to oils for anointing candles with, and they can be added to herb sachets, all of which we look at in our practical magic sections under each planet.

The choice of Tarot correspondences

I have included one or more Tarot (Major Arcana) in each of the planetary sections just to give you a flavour of the planet. They tell us something more about the characteristics and qualities of each planet and will enable you to get a sense of how to go deeper into each one. Although I have been learning Tarot for many years now, I do not profess to be an expert on the Tarot, and Tarot professionals – who may work with modern astrological correspondences instead of the pre-modern planetary rulers – may disagree with the cards I have selected. That is ok – this is not a book about Tarot, I simply include a brief description of the cards (as I see them) to illustrate the energy of the planets. These are a starting place only. If it is an area you are interested in, I would encourage you to go and explore more fully in a tarot class or a good book (I have included one in my list of further reading sources at the end).

The Source Texts are Full of Contradictions

Do expect to find conflicting lists of correspondences in lots of different places. I have focused largely on Cornelius Agrippa here, as his is one of the earlier sources for planetary correspondences, and if you look at other grimoires like *The Magus*, or books of Herbal Medicine like Nicolas Culpepper, they all quote the same systems, but you may well find some contradictions. Even Agrippa contradicts himself in a few places (bay leaves are under the Moon, but laurel is also under the sun.) I once read online that the colour of the Moon was purple, which I scoffed at and dismissed as ridiculous. Later, slightly red-faced I realised that in the tradition of Kabbalah, Hod (the Sephiroth of the Moon) is purple. You will also discover that in some sources, mint herbs are associated with the planet Venus, whereas I prefer to list them amongst Mercury's herbs, as to me they evoke fresh ideas, not love, apart from apple mint, which has a sweeter and more gently scent which is more Venusian in feel. The important thing is to learn the sources, know where they came from and why, and then you can make up your own mind. It's also helpful to note what your sources are as it helps you get to grips with the differing information that sometimes appears – my own private books of magic note which correspondences came from Agrippa, *The Key of Solomon*, Nicolas Culpeper, Scott Cunningham etc. That way you can trace lines of concordance (which gives you a sense of how long something has been the case) and allows you to see where modern variations may have crept in.

Magical Timing and Planetary Days and Hours

When you do your magic is as important as how you perform your magic, and this is one area that Pre-Modern Planetary magic can really help you with. Magic can sometimes feel a bit like trying to get into the ocean when the waves are crashing all around you – you must go with the current, and not try to fight the tide. Timing your entry between the waves is essential. With planetary magic, we have a ready-made almanac of when the currents are moving in the right direction for a particular magical working. This is because each of the seven planets has a day that it rules, and in addition, each day is divided into planetary hours.

The figure below is taken from a Shepherd's Almanac from 1503. It shows us a plethora of information about the planets. The picture is intriguing to look at, as it gives you a window into another time, and it is also very instructive when you begin to decode it.

I often spend some time in my classes asking my students to tell me what they see in this picture, and every time someone sees something I have not noticed before. It is like a police line-up of the seven planets, and each mug shot tells us something about how each planet .operates as an individual power, as well as part of the collective seven. The first thing students normally notice is that the days of the week are not in order. In classical astronomy, the planets are ordered according to the earth-centric world view. If we read from the right-hand side, you will notice the first planet is the Moon, which is closest to Earth. However, in the West we are taught to read from left to right, so if we begin there, you might notice the planetary line-up starts with Saturn on the left and works through the sequence to Lunar on the right. This is known as the Chaldean sequence – a system of numerology that comes from Ancient Babylon (625–539 BCE) whereby we begin with the planet that is furthest away from Earth, and the one that has the slowest orbit (Saturn) and work back to the nearest and fastest (the Moon).

We can also see the day of the week attributed to the planet, as well as any astrological signs that fall under it. And each planetary power stands in its own unique way – Venus holds a hand mirror, since she is the planet of beauty, while her groin is covered with a star, as that is how she appears in the night sky. Mars wears a helmet and carries a shield and a banner of war, also covering his modesty with a star, while the sun wears a solar disc and is flanked by the symbol for the astrological sign of Leo. We'll refer to this illustration later, so it is worth bookmarking this page.

Decoding the planetary ruler for each day is as simple as a name. If you are an English speaker, you might be scratching your head at this point, but translate the names into French, Spanish, Portuguese, or Italian (known as the romance languages), and things become much clearer. That is because the romance languages are rooted in Latin, and they were named for the Roman pantheon, which gives us our planetary names as well. The English names for the days of the week were named for the Norse pantheon.

Days of the week in English include things like Thursday, or Thor's Day, or Wednesday (Woden's Day) whereas in French it becomes Jeudi (Jove's Day), Mercredi (Mercury's Day), Mardi (Mars' Day), Vendredi (Venus's day). This tells us then, that if you want to do a spell for Venus, the best day to do it is on a Friday. A spell for Mars should be done on Tuesday, and so on.

But what about planetary hours? Under the Chaldean system, each day is also divided into planetary hours. The first hour of the day after sunrise is always attributed to the planet of the day, so dawn on Friday is the hour of Venus. However, these are not hours of sixty minutes, as we are accustomed to as daylight hours differ on each day of the solar year. The daylight hours need to be divided up equally between the seven. If you want to understand the mathematical equation involved, I recommend reading D'Este and Rankine's book of *Practical Planetary Magick*, which eloquently sets out the maths.

As this is an introductory book, and meant to be kept concise, I will say one thing – there's an app for that! Astrological apps can tell you exactly what the hour is, and even set an alarm on your phone for you. If you are not a slave to a smartphone, then you can also check on the internet.

By marrying up the planetary hour and day, you can increase the potency of the planetary power going into your spell work, blending the planets like a perfume, thereby increasing the subtlety of your magic. Want to do a spell for more sex in your life? Then cast a spell on Friday at the hour of Mars to give yourself a love spell with a hint of fiery passion. Want to uncover the reason for your writer's block? Then cast a Lunar spell at the hour of Mercury on a Monday.

The Illustrations

All the illustrations in the book are taken from pre-modern woodcuts from either the grimoire tradition, or medieval tomes on the nature of the universe. They each give us a unique window on how the ancient universe was constructed. Many of them show the planetary powers in anthropomorphic form and enable us to decode some of the traditional correspondences that were attributed to each of the powers. They are a useful resource in deepening your relationship with the planetary powers.

The Orphic Hymns

You will see I have included the Orphic Hymns in each chapter. For those of you that need to know such details, these are the 1792 translations by Thomas Taylor. They have obviously been supplanted by newer versions since then, but the Taylor edition is readily available (and open source). If you want to work with a more contemporary version, I've referenced one in the further reading section at the back.

Are you eager to now meet the planets? First, then, let us meet Madame de la Luna.

Chapter 3

Creating Moon Magic

Hear, Goddess queen, diffusing silver light,
Bull-horn'd and wand'ring thro' the gloom of Night.
With stars surrounded, and with circuit wide
Night's torch extending, thro' the heav'ns you ride:
Female and Male with borrow'd rays you shine,
And now full-orb'd, now tending to decline.
Mother of ages, fruit-producing Moon,
Whose amber orb makes Night's reflected noon:
Lover of horses, splendid, queen of Night,
All-seeing pow'r bedeck'd with starry light.
Lover of vigilance, the foe of strife,
In peace rejoicing, and a prudent life:
Fair lamp of Night, its ornament and friend,
Who giv'st to Nature's works their destin'd end.
Queen of the stars, all-wife Diana hail!
Deck'd with a graceful robe and shining veil;
Come, blessed Goddess, prudent, starry, bright,
Come moony-lamp with chaste and splendid light,
Shine on these sacred rites with prosp'rous rays,
And pleas'd accept thy suppliant's mystic praise.
(Orphic Hymn VIII to The Moon[5])

An Introduction to Madame de la Luna

As long as humans have walked the earth, they have gazed up in wonder at the night sky, watching the moon go through her twenty-eight-day cycle. From dark moon, to waxing moon, to full moon to waning moon and back round again – an endless cycle of growth, fullness, waning, death and rebirth. As Henry Bertram Law Webb wrote in 1911 in his book, *The Silences of the Moon,*

The millions of pensive mortal eyes that have gazed upon her, the thousands of passionate-speaking mortal lips that have sung to her, have given her this accumulative personality of infinite tenderness and delicacy... To step into moonlight is to step into the presence of a god; sorrow which has ached for what seemed many ages, melts away at the touch of so rich a maturity, so deep an experience; it is as though in the midst of our whimpering, we were suddenly confronted by the Mater Dolorosa.[6]

We know from science that the moon governs the tides, moving the boundless oceans in their own wave-cycle, and it also governs women's cycles. Even though we like to think we live in a logical, well-ordered world, the moon cannot help but affect us deeply, often on an unconscious level (we are made up of 60% water after all). It is not hard to see, then, the pre-modern concepts of the things that fall under the moon.

It is not just the Modern Pagan faiths that follow the cycles of the moon – other religions also follow lunar calendars. The ancient Babylonians followed a lunar calendar, the Jewish calendar is also a lunar one. Also, the beginning and end of Ramadan is determined by the placement of the new Moon, so Muslims the world over watch and wait for the appearance of the new moon to determine what day Eid will fall on. Christianity also has some lunar influences – the day ascribed for Easter each year is determined it being the first Sunday after the full Moon that occurs on or after the Spring Equinox.

Working with Moon Phases

Witches determine our magical workings by the cycles of the moon. The Witches' calendar is made up of eight Sabbats that celebrate the traditional cycles of nature, and thirteen Esbats across the year. The Esbats are when we come together in our coven groups and work magic. As Doreen Valiente's version of 'The Charge of the Goddess' tells us,

> *Whenever ye have need of anything, once in the month and better it be when the Moon is full, then shall ye assemble in some secret place, and call upon me, whom am Queen of all witcheries.*[7]

If the witch's path has chosen you, following the moon cycles is a good place to start your magical practice. The internet is full of apps that will help you to do this, effortlessly tracking the moon's cycles, so that even if you live in the most light-polluted parts of the city, you can time your magical workings to the correct cycle of the moon. But just what are those cycles?

New or Waxing Moon – currently the moon is growing. Well, in truth, the moon does not change size at all, but what we see from our world changes as Earth dances around the sun. From where we stand, the moon looks like it is growing and shrinking in size. While the moon is waxing, it appears to be increasing a little more each day. Waxing moon is the time for working magic which is bringing something to you.

Full Moon – is the most powerful day of the lunar cycle. It is that moment in time when the moon appears full, and we work most of our magic. If something is important to you, and is potentially life changing, then make sure you carry out the work at the full moon. This is also the traditional time to celebrate the Moon's cycles themselves, by holding a ceremony (or esbat) to mark this, either alone at your altar or in company with friends.

Waning Moon – when the moon appears to shrink in size, then work the magic that is sending things away from you. If you want to shake off that addiction, or that pattern of self-destructive behaviour, then the waning moon is the time to do this.

We often talk in terms of there being three phases of the moon, but I tend to add a fourth, which is sometimes passed over and forgotten about:

Dark Moon – when the Moon has vanished from sight, and it is no longer visible in the night sky, this is the time for introspective work, for example, time with your journal or your oracle deck, or by resting to replenish your own energy levels. It is a time for self-care, rest, and reflection. Following nature's cycles in life, also means you must honour your own cycles, and listen to your own body. You can only do this by being quiet and relaxing from time to time, a skill that is particularly crucial if you are living in the fast, frenetic atmosphere of a city where life never stops for a second.

If we want to work with the Moon as a planetary power, just what qualities are attributed to it? Again, looking at a medieval woodcut (such as the one from the Shepherd's Almanac) we start to pick out the clues. But just in case you are busy with a day job and a family and a social life, and you don't have hours to decode old medieval woodcuts, I will also give you a few tips.

Guido Bonatti's Moon illustration (1297) shows us the Moon riding in her chariot across clouds or the sea, being drawn by two maidens, showing the sign of Cancer on the wheel, and a sea serpent at her feet. In her hand is her hunting spear, on her head the lunar crown.

Lunar Symbols and Sigils

We start with the most commonly used symbol for the moon – the simple crescent which comes from the alchemical and astrological traditions. This is used as shorthand for the Moon.

You may have also encountered the triple moon symbol on your travels – this one expresses the three phases of the moon and is often seen on jewellery and other items. Aside from the traditional crescent moon, or triple moon images, there are some other symbols you can work with if you want to call upon the moon's energies.

How do you work with all these sigils? They can be carved onto candles with a cocktail stick or a pencil or drawn on paper that is then included in an herb sachet or drawn onto a tablet of air-drying clay if you are doing sigil magic. The possibilities are endless. Remember – these symbols are there to help you communicate to your unconscious mind what you want it to do for you. It's a way of pre-programming your RAS.

Agrippa's Lunar Magic

In Agrippa's kamea for the Moon, there are 9 rows and columns, containing 81 numbers in total. Each row, column or diagonal adds up to 369. The entire kamea one adds up to 3,321. This means if you are wanting top to perform lunar magic, you might want to incorporate a lunar number in some way. For example, 9 drops of jasmine essential oil in a recipe, or 9 days to carry out a spell.

37	78	29	70	21	62	13	54	5
6	38	79	30	71	22	63	14	46
47	7	39	80	31	72	23	55	15
16	48	8	40	81	32	64	24	56
57	17	49	9	41	73	33	65	25
26	58	18	50	1	42	74	34	66
67	27	59	10	51	2	43	75	35
36	68	19	60	11	52	3	44	76
77	28	69	20	61	12	53	4	45

Agrippa's seal of the moon is shown below.

Agrippa's Lunar Suffumigation

Agrippa tells us 'to the Moon, the leaves of all vegetables, as the leaf indium, and the leaves of the myrtle and bay-tree'. He goes on to say,

> For the Moon we make a suffumigation of the head of a Frog dried, the eyes of a Bull, the seed of white Poppy, Frankincense, and Camphor, which must be incorporated with Menstruous blood, or the blood of a Goose.[8]

Agrippa is telling us that the animals associated with the Moon are the frog, the bull, and the goose, while the herbs are the soporifics – poppy, camphor, frankincense, and that menstrual blood is a powerful link to the moon. I would always avoid the animal derived products and leave our non-human animal companions safely outside of the recipe for magical workings. Here is my recipe as an alternative (adding your own menstrual blood is entirely optional, and gives a powerful link between you and your magical aim):

A Lunar Incense for Scrying or Divination

To burn an incense, you will need a censor – a heatproof container (either a metal thurible, or an old mug or earthenware dish). Fill it to 1cm below the top with earth, salt, or sand. You will also need some small charcoal discs – the type used in shisha pipes, so you will find these in a local international supermarket, or online. It is also useful to have a pestle and mortar for this, to grind the ingredients together.

You will need:

1 tablespoon of frankincense pearls
9 jasmine flowers
9 drops of Sandalwood oil

9 drops of Jasmine oil

9 drops of Camphor oil

On a Monday, or on a full moon, at the hour of the Moon, begin by grinding the dried jasmine blossoms in a pestle and mortar, then add the resin, and finally the essential oils. As you mix, think about the successful scrying / divination session you want to have. You can read aloud the Orphic Hymn to the Moon as you mix, and when you feel the energy within you reach a pinnacle, say the words, 'and so it is'.

Fill the censor with salt or sand and place a lit charcoal disc on top (you may also like to use tweezers or sugar tongs for handling the charcoal to prevent burns). When the charcoal starts to turn grey in colour, it is ready for use. Sprinkle on the incense, making sure you keep the windows open, and the room well aired. It's also best to keep your feathered and furred folk in another room.

As the incense smoke goes skyward, think about the Moon's energies surrounding you.

Lunar Deities

If the Graeco-Roman Pantheon is not one that resonates for you, then never fear. That doesn't make you a crap witch. There are other pantheons out there that you can develop a good working relationship with, and there are plenty of different lunar deities to choose from, and they are often easy to spot as they will often wear the horned crowns that look like a crescent moon. In each case I will give you three of four suggestions, to start you off on your explorations. The following Goddesses may give you a starting point for the Moon:

Diana / Artemis

Diana is the Roman, while Artemis is the Greek embodiment of the lunar goddess. Often portrayed as the huntress, carrying her bow, and accompanied by her hunting dogs, she represents the moon in her maiden aspect (we often see Lunar goddesses as either their Maiden, Mother or Crone aspect). Suitable offerings to Diana / Artemis might include frankincense, nuts, mugwort, and music or dance.

Hathor

Hathor is the Egyptian 'great goddess of many names' and is often depicted with a cow's head or horns, or with a woman's face but with cow ears. Hathor is the goddess of childbirth and motherhood and was closely linked to Isis (who later became merged with her). She is known as the mistress of life and governed music, dance, love, and she also protected the dead on their final journey to the underworld. Suitable offerings for Hathor might include malachite, myrrh, milk, and two mirrors.

Hecate

Hecate is one of the few lunar goddesses to appear in a Shakespeare play. In Macbeth, the witches meet with her as she is Queen of the Witches, and she admonishes them for giving Macbeth the prophesies without informing her. In this aspect, Hecate is formidable, but she also has a kinder side. Often depicted as a goddess who stands at the crossroads, holding aloft her lantern to light the way. But she is also depicted with three faces or three bodies (the three phases of the moon) and is accompanied by her fierce pack of hounds. Hecate was associated with herb lore, so if this is an area that interests you, she would be a worthy companion.

Mani

Mani is a male lunar deity who comes from Germanic mythology. He is mentioned in both the *Poetic Edda* and the *Prose Edda*, as the brother of the Sun god, Sól. Some scholars link him to the Northern Hemisphere's perception of the man in the moon.

The Poetic Edda recounts how Mani and his sister, Sól are pursued through the heavens by wolves. Sól seeks shelter in the protecting woods through the night, while Mani continues to be chased. In the *Prose Edda*, it is told that Mani guides the path of the Moon and controls its phases.

Lunar Tarot

The High Priestess

The High Priestess sits, protected by her cloak, and crowned by the three phases of the Moon. She is linked to Persephone, the goddess of the Underworld by her links with pomegranate seeds, and in some decks, she is the source of the stream that runs through many of the other cards. She represents a deep stirring within the self, a subtle but powerful connection to the collective unconscious, and an inspired state of being. She brings surges of wisdom that benefit any creative endeavour – artistic, scientific, or esoteric. She can represent seeking guidance and knowledge, seclusion and self-reliance, good judgement, and psychic ability. Receptivity and meditation can bring new situations to light.

The Moon Card

The Moon card in Tarot is the card of the imagination, as it moulds the energy of the unconscious into shapes the conscious can understand. Myths are often distorted – they can never clearly state what we want, but they can appeal to what lies deep within the hidden self. While the Sun shines its own light, the Moon can only reflect the hidden light of the sun.

Because the Moon represents the unknown depths, unconscious activity, emotions, illusion, and bewilderment, it can have an eerie presence, and evokes strange feelings in people and animals. It can often indicate a period of introspection, of obscurity and searching for the hidden truth that lies beneath the surface. It can also indicate a need to guard against influence and deception, and a struggle to distinguish between reality and illusion. However, a balance of intuition, imagination and intellect can bring great wisdom.

Practical Lunar Magic

A Recipe for Lunar Bath Salts

In magical terms, salt is a cleanser of all things energetic. In Wicca, we use salt and water to cleanse the room and ourselves of any residual energy before casting a circle and carrying out any magical work. That way, you are not taking anything into sacred space except your highest intentions. One way to cleanse yourself is to take a ritual bath before undertaking magical work.

Making your own sacred bath salts at home couldn't be any easier. On a Monday or on a Full Moon, simply mix together:

One cup of sea salt
One half cup of Epsom salts (you can buy these at chemists as they are good for muscle aches)
A half cup of Bicarbonate of Soda (to soften the water and your skin. You will find this in the baking section of your supermarket)
Nine drops of jasmine essential oil
Nine drops of sandalwood essential oil
Twenty-eight Jasmin blossoms (available online or from an herbalist)

As you add the essential oils to the salt, rub them in to the mix to disperse them throughout the salts. Once you have mixed the ingredients together, keep your Lunar bath salts in a glass screw top jar, and add three tablespoons to warm running water. As you do so, visualise the moons rays shining down on the water, light some candles and really relax in the moon's glow.

Lunar Tea for Dreaming

For this you will need either a good old-fashioned tea pot, a tea infuser, a tea strainer, or a packet of re-fillable tea bags (otherwise you will be chewing your tea, which is never a good look). Take:

    9 Mugwort leaves
    9 Jasmine blossoms
    9 pieces of dried lemon peel

Add the herbs to your teapot or infuser, pour on boiled water, and leave it to steep for 9 minutes. While it is infusing, stir and picture the Moon's positive influence in your life.

Full Moon Oil

This recipe can be used for anointing yourself, your divination tools or lunar crystals, or your candles in candle magic. On a Monday (or under a full Moon), mix:

    9 drops of Frankincense oil
    9 drops Sandalwood oil
    9 drops Jasmine oil
    Half a cup of coconut oil (you will need to warm this in warm water each time you want to use it as it will go solid).
    A piece of moonstone

As you mix, visualise the successful outcome you are working for – successful divination, pregnancy, prophetic dreaming etc, whatever endeavour you need a dose of Lunar success for. Leave the oil on a windowsill overnight in the light of the Full moon. Then use it to anoint you, the item you want to bring a successful result in, or to anoint a candle for a candle spell.

Making a Full Moon Lunar Talisman

A lot of successful practical magic requires that you access the child-like aspects of yourself and believe in a world of wonder again. That is because you are working with your unconscious mind, which is in effect a seven-year-old child. Many of the practical magical exercises I give you in this book will tap into that inner child. So, if you feel like you are back at school in the arts and crafts class or at playtime, that's fine. That's the part of you we are trying to access, so just enjoy it, let go and tell your conscious mind to put the running commentary on pause for a while.

To make a lunar talisman, we are going to work with air drying clay and silver paint, and work the spell over three nights, beginning the work two nights before the full moon (so that the third night is the night of the full moon).

You will need:

A block of air-drying clay (this can usually be bought online or in a budget stationery supplier, or at an art supplies shop)
Some silver paint – acrylic is best – and a brush
A cocktail stick
A moonstone or other appropriate lunar crystal
A symbol of your relevant intent (for example, if your intent is to foster your ability to read the tarot, have a tarot deck with you.
A large round white plate
A rolling pin or glass

Begin by clarifying for yourself exactly what your intent is for the spell. If your thoughts are not clear, the result will be likewise muddied, and, just like our SMART goals at work, that intention needs to be stated in the positive, timed, measurable and phrased as if it is now. For example,

'It is January 2023, and I can read the tarot cards easily and effortlessly'.

As you work the clay with your hands, keep that intention foremost in your mind.

On the first night, take a golf-ball sized piece of clay and roll it in your hands as you continuously state your intention. Then place it on the white plate and flatten it into a round tablet shape. (You can roll it out like you would dough, using the side of a glass if you don't own a rolling pin).

Once you have the round shape rolled out, place the moonstone at the centre, and, using the cocktail stick carve out a moon sigil on the flat surface, and your initials. At this point, allow yourself a little playtime with the design – it can be as simple or as elaborate as you would like it to be. Once you are happy with the design, set the plate to one side to allow the clay to dry (for example overnight). If you can leave it out under the light of the waxing moon, all the better, and place with it the symbol of your intent (e.g., the tarot deck).

On the second night, once the clay has dried, it is time to then paint the tablet silver. Again, as you paint, allow yourself a little playfulness, and continue to think of your intent. Set the tablet aside and allow the paint to dry, again, under the light of the moon and with the symbol of your intent if you can.

On the third night, your tablet is ready to be charged up fully with your intent. Take the symbol of your intent and place it in front of you next to the candle. Light the candle, stating your intent clearly and in the now again. Take up the clay tablet and hold it in your hand. Repeat your statement of intent again three times. As you repeat the statement of intent, feel the warmth from your hands transferring into the tablet, and allow that energy to flow. When that energy has reached its peak, complete the spell with the statement, 'And so it is!'

You can now carry the lunar sigil with you, or better still, keep it with the symbol or tool of your intent so that you can draw on its energy each time you need to. Now that you have your talisman, you need to do work on the mundane plane to help the spell do its work. You see, the thing that most people don't understand with magic is that you must help it along – it's not enough to do a spell and then expect it all to come to you with no help from you! Now you have to put yourself in the way of opportunities to help the magic do its work.

Lunar Correspondences

Each of the correspondence tables throughout the book has been put together in my reading of the grimoires that I read during my magical training. I have added to them as the years have moved on and I have made other discoveries along the witches' path. In each case I have tried to be as varied as I can be – the Grimoires give us lists of herbs, crystals, and foods we can work with, as well as qualities that the planetary power holds. This gives us quite a varied way of working with them. You might choose to hold a planetary themed evening on the appropriate day of the week (in this case Monday) where you eat the foods that are governed by the moon, burning silver candles, and reading aloud the various poems or prose that has been written by those inspired by its wondrous beauty. Throughout the chapters I have also included some of my favourite quotes from literature since that is the lens through which I tend to look.

Another way you might celebrate the Moon, is by building an altar to it, which you may furnish with pictures, and poems, of little animal statues, appropriate crystals, and candles and herbs. The best way to grow a spiritual practice is to do what you are drawn to instinctively. That way your spiritual life becomes a source of joy, and not one of drudgery. It will help you by freeing up your creative energies, and not blocking them. If you are drawn to crystals, work with the crystal correspondences. If you are already a practiced tarot practitioner, work with the cards that are attributed to the Moon. If you love cooking, explore the ways you can express yourself through recipes using lunar foods (or do all the above).

Chapter 4

Creating Mercury Magic

Hermes, draw near, and to my pray'r incline,
Angel of Jove, and Maia's son divine;
Studious of contests, ruler of mankind,
With heart almighty, and a prudent mind.
Celestial messenger, of various skill,
Whose pow'rful arts could watchful Argus kill:
With winged feet, 'tis thine thro' air to course,
O friend of man, and prophet of discourse:
Great life-supporter, to rejoice is thine,
In arts gymnastic, and in fraud divine:
With pow'r endu'd all language to explain,
Of care the loos'ner, and the source of gain.
Whose hand contains of blameless peace the rod,
Corucian, blessed, profitable God;
Of various speech, whose aid in works we find,
And in necessities to mortals kind:
Dire weapon of the tongue, which men revere,
Be present, Hermes, and thy suppliant hear;
Assist my works, conclude my life with peace,
Give graceful speech, and me memory's increase.
(Orphic Hymn XXVII to Hermes[9])

A Mercurial Introduction

Mercury represents the forces of all things changeable. It is our trickster among the planets, and it is also our most gender fluid planet. It is above all else mutable, never to be pinned down or tamed (unless it wants to be). It also has a wicked sense of humour and will deliver your magical request with a flourish and a swift kick in the pants. You will notice my avoidance of gendered pronouns – that is because Mercury (in my experience) is fluid in every sense. It sometimes appears as male, but also sometimes as non-binary.

Working with Mercury is not for the faint-hearted. Mercury is not only the ruling planet of communication and travel, but in its god / planet cross over, they are also the Roman equivalent of Loki, the trickster god of the North. When you start working with Mercury, don't be surprised if arrangements go awry and things go missing – Mercury is after all the planetary ruler of pickpockets, as well as banking and merchants. If you ask Mercury to bring wealth to you, it will as likely vanish as fast as it arrived. If, however, you want to improve your trade, your eloquence, or your ability write well, then Mercury is your planet.

Mercury's animals give a hint to the qualities of the planet. If we think back to childhood stories, such as *Aesop's Fables*, *Fantastic Mr Fox*, *The Wind in the Willows*, and a host of other folkloric tales, they often include foxes, corvids or weasels who are renowned for their cunning, and sometimes up to no good. Mercury is the loveable rogue that you might choose not to take home to meet your family, but secretly you harbour a lot of love for.

Mercury Retrograde, or WTF just happened?

All our planets can go into a retrograde phase at one time or another. This is an astrological phenomenon whereby the planet *appears* to be travelling backwards in the sky, although it is not. It's all down to perspective from Earth. When a planet enters a retrograde phase, it can bring unexpected results, as it reverses the polarity of the planetary energy.

Mercury Retrograde is just one of those periods. You will probably have read about it somewhere, as it's been picked up by mainstream media in recent years. When Mercury goes Retrograde (MRx in shorthand) there are said to be problems that manifest – for instance, travel problems (cancelled trains, broken down cars, plane delays), computer break downs, communication errors, you send that awful email to the wrong person and then find yourself squirming. It's worth being extra aware of what you are communicating and to whom during a retrograde phase, as these are the times Mercury goes full trickster.

However, there is also a deeper level of introspection that can occur. If you sit tight and don't get too het up about having to slow down, Mercury Retrograde can also bring some interesting introspections, which are usually coloured by the house or star sign they are retrograde in. For example, Mercury Retrograde in Aries may cause sudden arguments, but it might also help you to find the hidden assertiveness you need to really express the opinion you've been struggling to find the words for. Mercury Retrograde in Pisces can make for some trippy introspection. Mercury retrograde in Taurus might lead you to think about your home or love life, and how you want to arrange things differently.

Working with Mercury

If Mercury always comes with a little warning, and is tricky to work with, how can we try and tame it? My NLP teacher would give us a clue here by reminding me that the work 'try' presupposes failure. Don't *try* to tame Mercury at all, just roll with the adventure of working with this most lively of planets. After spending years building up a relationship with Mercury, I can mostly channel its energies successfully, but even now, it can always surprise me. While all magic can often be delivered with a humorous flourish, Mercury is the most obvious planet that behaves in this way. If we have a look at its correspondences, you will begin to see why. Always expect the unexpected when working with Mercury.

How do we capture mercury in our Spell craft? Spells that encompass air or movement – incenses, knot magic, and chanting (as it is using voice, language, and air).

Mercurial Symbols and Sigils

Mercury can be symbolised in several different ways. You

can either use the alchemical glyph for Mercury, which is reminiscent of the divine feminine in its use of the Venus glyph combined with the horned crown of the Moon or wearing the winged helmet of Mercury / Hermes.

Another symbol frequently used to represent Mercury is the Caduceus wand – the wand entwined with two snakes; a movement seen in the natural world when two snakes come together to mate. Its use dates to before the Romans, and is a symbol seen all over the globe – in Ancient Mesopotamia, Egypt, India amongst others. It has become confused with the Asclepius wand (which depicts only a single snake) and so has been used as the symbol for the US Medical Corps, pharmacies, and Health related professions. More appropriate to Mercury perhaps, it is also employed by commerce related industries.

Guido Bonatti's illustration shows Mercury riding in a chariot drawn by two birds (his association with the element of air), with his astrological signs – Gemini and Virgo – are depicted on the wheels. In his hand, of course, he holds the caduceus wand.

The snake symbolism is a common theme in folklore – it often represents transformation (the shedding of skins), knowledge, fertility, rebirth, and immortality. It's about growth and change, and the inner knowledge and wisdom that comes from that process.

Agrippa's Mercurial Magic

Moving swiftly on to Agrippa's magic of numbers, Mercury's kamea employs the numbers 8 (the rows and columns) and 64 (the square contains 64 numbers in total). While each row or column adds up to 260, all the numbers sum 2,080. These then, are all appropriate numbers for Mercurial Magic. Work them into your spells by using 8 as your base number – 8 drops of oil, 8 leaves of an herb, 8 candles, etc.

8	58	59	5	4	62	63	1
49	15	14	52	53	11	10	56
41	23	22	44	45	19	18	48
32	34	35	29	28	38	39	25
40	26	27	37	36	30	31	33
17	47	46	20	21	43	42	24
9	55	54	12	13	51	50	16
64	2	3	61	60	6	7	57

Agrippa's Seal of Mercury can be used in spells involving parchment, candle magic or written on the body in paint, oil or any substance of your choosing. The marvellous thing about planetary magic is that you will never run out of ideas about how to apply it. From body paint to underwear, from scarves to hats, from spell pouches to candle spells, the possible combinations are infinite.

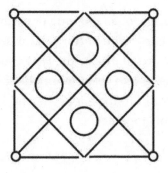

Agrippa's Mercury Suffumigation

Agrippa writes that, 'to Mercury, all the peels of wood and fruit, as cinnamon, lignum cassia, mace, citron or lemon peel'. He also gives us one of his usual delights in his recipes for his suffumigation. Agrippa tells us,

> For Mercury, take mastic, frankincense, cloves, and the herb cinquefoil, and the stone achate, and incorporate them all with the brain of a fox or weasel, and the blood of a magpie. [8]

Fortunately, we don't still follow these recipes today, and you are unlikely to encounter a supplier of fox brains, or magpie blood, but it's worth noting, that these ingredients are listed by Agrippa because they are all animals who fall under the dominion of Mercury. Foxes, corvids, and weasels are renowned for their cunning, and this gives you more clues as to the qualities of Mercury. It's their mental agility, their quick thinking and their speed that can be so useful in Mercurial spells. If you need fast results, Mercury is your go-to planet of choice.

Here's my cruelty-free version of a Mercurial Incense.

A Mercurial Incense for Clarity, Free-Movement and to Remove Obstacles

To burn an incense, you will need a censor – a heatproof container (either a metal thurible, or an old mug or earthenware dish). Fill it to 1cm below the top with earth, salt, or sand. You will also need some small charcoal discs – the type used in shisha pipes, so you will find these in a local international supermarket, or online. It is also useful to have a pestle and mortar for this, to grind the ingredients together.

You will need:

A dessert spoon of frankincense pearls
Half a dessert spoon of lavender flowers
Half a dessert spoon of dried fennel
6 drops of bergamot essential oil
6 drops of lavender essential oil

On a Wednesday, or at the hour of Mercury, begin by grinding the dried flowers in a pestle and mortar, then add the resin, and finally the essential oils. As you mix, think about the way in front of you becoming clear, and your ability to move towards your goal freely. You can even read aloud the Orphic Hymn as you mix, and when you feel the energy within you reach a peak, say the words, 'So mote it be', or if you prefer something a little less archaic, 'so be it'.

Fill the censor with salt or sand and place a lit charcoal disc on top (you may also like to use tweezers or sugar tongs for handling the charcoal to prevent burns). When the charcoal starts to turn grey in colour, it is ready for use. Sprinkle on the incense, making sure you keep the windows open, and the room well aired. It's also best to keep your feathered and furred folk in another room.

As the incense smoke goes skyward, think about Mercury delivering your message to the universe.

Mercurial Deities

Loki

One of the Norse pantheon, Loki is neither good nor evil in their stories – their main aim is often to create chaos, but as we know, sometimes pandemonium can bring creativity. Loki is well known for their trickster activities, but also for their ingenious problem-solving abilities. While they get the other gods into trouble, they often find imaginative solutions too. Loki is written about in the *Poetic Edda*, a collection of tales about the Norse pantheon which was compiled in the 13th Century from older sources, and they are also present in many contemporary stories – from Marvel comics' portrayal of Loki and Thor to Neil Gaiman's fabulous re-telling of Norse Mythology and American Gods. Just like his Roman and Greek counterparts, Loki can switch gender at will, and is interpreted by modern scholars as gender fluid. They are a good deity to work with if you want to tap into your own creativity and your ability to think quickly.

Ganesh

Ganesh is one of the best loved of all the gods. He hails from the Hindu pantheon, and has the body of a man, and the head of an elephant. He is the god of beginnings, and the remover of obstacles. Born in human form, he is the son of Parvati. In some tales, Shiva (or one of his attendants) was jealous of Parvati's love for Ganesh, and so cut off his head. He was then given an elephant's head in order that he could live. He is often depicted with a mouse or a rat (symbolising his ability to gnaw through any problem), a lotus (symbolising divine energy and the ability to start afresh every day), and a broken tusk (which he uses to write).

Hermaphroditus

Hermaphroditus is a conflation of their parents, Hermes, and Aphrodite. Hermaphroditus was originally part of the Greek pantheon, and their earliest worship traces back to Cyprus, but there was also a temple to Hermaphroditus in Athens. Hermaphrodite's myths are written about in Ovid's *Metamorphosis*. Often depicted as a beautiful maiden with male genitalia, Hermaphrodite was born a beautiful boy and raised by nymphs on Mount Ida. Setting out to conquer the world with his beauty, at the age of 15 he travelled to Caria, where he encountered the nymph Salmacis sitting near a fountain. Hermaphroditus rejected Salmacis's advances, and, frustrated by unrequited passion, she waited until the boy was bathing naked in a pool, surprised him with a passionate embrace, and cried out to the gods to join the two of them together forever. The gods relented, and so Hermaphroditus the non-binary deity was created.

Papa Legba

Some of our god's cousins and counterparts can be related to more than one planet, and Papa Legba is one of these. Sometimes he also carries aspects of Saturn (particularly in his appearance), but I think he is also mercurial in nature. He is a Lwa (pronounced lowa) in Haitian Vodou, a spirit who serves the Creator god. Papa Legba is a shape shifter, and he acts as an intermediary between humans and the Lwa, and the bridge between the spirit world and the world of humans. He is invoked at the beginning of Vodou ceremonies to enable the other Lwa to come in. He is found at the crossroads – that in-between place which is so favoured by many magical practitioners of all faiths. The reason I have listed him under Mercury is that, as well as representing liminality, he is said to speak all human languages. His origins are in the Dahomey faith from West Africa, and has a similar cousin in Legba, a Yoruban deity from Nigeria. Papa Legba shares Mercury and Loki's trickster energy, but also Ganesh's ability to open the gates and clear away obstacles. Offerings to Papa Legba include white rum, black coffee, and mangoes.

Mercurial Tarot

The Magician
The Magician has all their tools laid out in front of them, and they are poised like a lightning rod between the worlds of deity and mortals. Their energy is never depleted, they know what needs to be done, and how to do it – they just need to put will into action. The Magician represents consciousness, action, creation, and manifestation. They create the world using the four elements in front of them, but they also remind us that without action, and making something of the possibilities which are in front of us, it's all just ideas that do not really exist.

The Magician can represent skill and wisdom, and the noble use of your talents. It can mean being in a state of harmony with your environment, of being in possession of the power and influence, with an awareness of unseen powers. Reversed it can mean a draining of your energy, empty showmanship, and a loss of direction. A negative use of power, or just a manipulating trickster.

The Lovers
For a card that is Mercurial in its nature, nothing is ever straightforward. While the Lovers can represent sexual love, and a literal blossoming of a romantic relationship, older Tarot decks often depicted the Lovers card as an older man who has been struck by Cupid's arrow and must make a choice between two loves. The card can indicate a valuable relationship between two partners – it is a dance, a connection on a higher plane as well as in the physical world. It can also indicate the harmonious flow of energy, giving a sense of comfort and ease. It may also indicate that choice that must be made between what is desired, and what is acceptable.

Practical Mercurial Magic

A Mercurial Spell for Freeing Yourself

On a windy Wednesday, take yourself out into nature to a high place – either a hilltop, or a bridge. Somewhere you can really feel the wind in your hair. As you walk, pluck a leaf here and there from the trees or bushes around you. As you pluck each one, state the name of the bad habit, self-destructive behaviour, or person that you wish to let go of. When you reach the high place, stand for a moment with your back to the wind, and clutch the leaves to your heart. Name each leaf again, and as you do, think about what you would like to replace it with. For example, if you want to be rid of that negative voice in your head, and replace it with a kind voice instead, state that aloud, and as you do, let the leaf fly in the wind.

When you have released all your leaves (either singly or together) return home and start to put your good new habits into practice.

A Recipe for Unblocking Oil

This recipe encompasses multiple planets, but I am including it here as it is one of my favourite recipes for clearing blockages and allowing you to move forwards. You will need:

Base Oil (Olive Oil)
10 drops orange oil (Sun)
10 drops Pine oil (Mars)
10 drops of Vetivert (Saturn)
1 spring dried sage (Jupiter)
1 sprig dried lavender (Mercury)
1 sprig Rosemary (Sun)
1 pinch salt
½ teaspoon of frankincense pearls (Sun)

Mix all the ingredients together whilst thinking of the freedom of movement you will have. Again, you might like to read aloud the Orphic Hymn to Mercury.

Mercurial Tea

For this you will need either a good old-fashioned tea pot, a tea infuser, a tea strainer, or a packet of re-fillable tea bags (otherwise you will be chewing your tea, which is never a good look). Take:

8 lemon verbena leaves
A teaspoon of lavender flowers
8 dried mint leaves

Add the herbs to your teapot or infuser, pour on boiled water, and leave it to steep for 8 minutes. While it is infusing, stir and picture Mercury's positive influence in your life.

Chapter 5

Creating Venus Magic

HEAV'NLY, illustrious, laughter-loving queen,
Sea-born, night-loving, of an awful mien;
Crafty, from whom necessity first came,
Producing, nightly, all-connecting dame:
'Tis thine the world with harmony to join,
For all things spring from thee, O pow'r divine.
The triple Fates are rul'd by thy decree,
And all productions yield alike to thee:
Whate'er the heav'ns, encircling all contain,
Earth fruit-producing, and the stormy main,
Thy sway confesses, and obeys thy nod,
Awful attendant of the brumal God:
Goddess of marriage, charming to the sight,
Mother of Loves, whom banquetings delight;
Source of persuasion, secret, fav'ring queen,
Illustrious born, apparent and unseen:
Spousal, lupercal, and to men inclin'd,
Prolific, most-desir'd, life-giving., kind:
Great sceptre-bearer of the Gods, 'tis thine,
Mortals in necessary bands to join;
And ev'ry tribe of savage monsters dire
In magic chains to bind, thro' mad desire.
Come, Cyprus-born, and to my pray'r incline,
Whether exalted in the heav'ns you shine,
Or pleas'd in Syria's temple to preside,
Or o'er th' Egyptian plains thy car to guide,
Fashion'd of gold; and near its sacred flood,
Fertile and fam'd to fix thy blest abode;
Or if rejoicing in the azure shores,

Near where the sea with foaming billows roars,
The circling choirs of mortals, thy delight,
Or beauteous nymphs, with eyes cerulean bright,
Pleas'd by the dusty banks renown'd of old,
To drive thy rapid, two-yok'd car of gold;
Or if in Cyprus with thy mother fair,
Where married females praise thee ev'ry year,
And beauteous virgins in the chorus join,
Adonis pure to sing and thee divine;
Come, all-attractive to my pray'r inclin'd,
For thee, I call, with holy, reverent mind.
(Orphic Hymn LIV to Venus[10])

Introductions to Venus: or the Differences Between Planets and Gods

I have been a dedicated priestess of Venus since my earliest beginnings on the path to witchcraft. When I look back, she had marked me out long before I found modern paganism. Am I talking about the planet or the Goddess here? The planetary powers are not quite the same as the gods they are named for, but sometimes there is a hair's breadth between them. The correspondences are the same for them both, but the mythos belongs to the goddess. Tales of Venus emerging from the foaming sea off the Greek island of Cyprus refer to the Goddess, not the planet. The planet gives us echoes of the deity it is named for. While I am a priestess of the Goddess Venus, the planet Venus is the one of the planetary seven which comes to me most naturally. I am drawn to its herbs and crystals, as organically as breathing.

Working with Venus

What does it rule? This planet is the one that you call on when you have a need for beauty or harmony. While it holds dominion over love, it's not just eros (the sexual, passionate kind). The Ancient Greek's classified the different forms of love, and they give a sense of the breadth of Venus' spheres of influence. Just as it rules eros, it also governs agape (unconditional love), as well as philia (friendship), storge (familial love) and philautia (self-love).

This means we call on it when we want to bring more love (of any kind) into our lives. Had a fight with your best friend? Then you can petition Venus to smooth over the cracks in the road back to friendship. Feeling frazzled and over worked to the point of self-neglect and burn out? Then you can call on Venus to help you to remember that you are no use to anyone unless you are well rested and cared for.

Venus also rules the love of all things beautiful – art works, self-care, personal grooming, but it also gives us the root for the word venereal. It is also the Empress in Tarot – the strong, confident woman who has mastered her creative expression, her sensuality, and her fertility (not just in terms of reproduction). She is surrounded by abundance and nature.

Venusian Symbols and Sigils
Venus' planetary glyph is the symbol for the universal feminine.

In medieval woodcuts, Venus is often depicted in the company of Cupid as he is about to fire his bow, holding a heart and an arrow, and with her astrological signs, Taurus, and Libra. In Guido Bonatti's depiction of 1297, she is also in a chariot being drawn by two birds, depicting her association with pigeons and doves. They are ruled by Venus as they tend to flock together in groups.

Agrippa's Venusian Magic

22	47	16	41	10	35	4
5	23	48	17	42	11	29
30	6	24	49	18	36	12
13	31	7	25	43	19	37
38	14	32	1	26	44	20
21	39	8	33	2	27	45
46	15	40	9	34	3	28

Agrippa's magical number square for Venus gives a square with 7 rows and columns (which tells us that the number for Venus is 7). There are 49 numbers in total. Each row and column add up to 175, and the Kamea adds up to 1,225 in total.

The seal of Venus is a useful one to use in candle spells, or to write on parchment for inclusion in herbal spell sachets. It was designed to bring the essence of the planet Venus into magical workings.

Agrippa's Venusian Suffumigation
Agrippa tells us that 'to Venus, sweet flowers, as roses, violets, saffron, and such like'. For his suffumigation, he tells us:

> For Venus take Musk, Amber, Lignum-aloes, red Roses, and red Corall, and make them up with the brain of Sparrows, and the blood of Pigeons.[8]

We can tell in this recipe that Agrippa's animals of Venus include sparrows and pigeons. Herbs or perfumes include musk, amber, lignum aloes, red roses and red coral is the 'stone' associated with Venus (we know it is a living creature now). For a twenty-first century cruelty-free version, here is my own recipe.

An incense to bring love
On a Friday (or at the hour of Venus) take:

1 tablespoon of damar pearls
half a tablespoon of myrrh
half a tablespoon of rose petals
7 drops of rose essential oil
7 drops of geranium essential oil

Begin by grinding the dried flowers in a pestle and mortar, then add the resin, and finally the essential oils. Fill a censor with salt or sand and place a lit charcoal disc on top. Sprinkle on the incense, making sure you keep the windows open, and the room well aired, and do not leave the censor unattended.

Venusian Deities

Venus's cousins and counterparts, simply put, are the deities associated with love and beauty. There is never an absolute correlation between the deities – there will aways be some aspects that differ – but if we look to the deities associated with love, there are many similarities.

Aphrodite

Aphrodite is the Ancient Greek goddess who pre-dates the Roman Venus. Although Venus and Aphrodite are often conflated into one deity, there are subtle differences. Aphrodite was associated with sexual love and beauty, but she was also worshipped as a goddess of seafaring, and of warfare. She was born of the sea foam that arose when Cronus cut his father Uranus' genitals off and threw them into the sea. Aphrodite also ruled marriage and was the patron deity of sex workers.

Scholars believe this goddess came to Ancient Greece from the Middle Eastern goddesses Ishtar and Astarte. She was married to the blacksmith god Hephaestus, but she fell in love with Ares, and had other lovers besides him.

Isis

Isis is the (sometimes) winged goddess of Ancient Egypt. Daughter of the earth god, Geb, and the sky goddess, Nut, she is also sister to Seth, Nephthys, and Osiris, who was also her husband. She is mother to the god Horus. Her worship began in Egypt, but, with the Roman invasion of Egypt, her worship spread across the Roman Empire as far as the British Isles. The river Thames (Thame-Isis in the Roman era) is still referred to as the Isis as it flows through Oxford, and there was said to be a temple to Isis on the land where St. Paul's Cathedral now stands. Isis was the goddess of magic and love, and she is associated with healing, bringing the dead back to life, and the patron deity of mothers.

Her most famous myth is the story of her bringing her husband Osiris back to life. He had been murdered by his brother Seth in a jealous rage, and then his body was cut into pieces and scattered across all of Egypt. Isis went in search of all the pieces, with the help of Nephthys, and was able to retrieve all but his phallus. Using her magic, she brought him back to life, replaced his missing penis with an artificial one, and bore him a son (Horus). Osiris then became the god of the Underworld.

Erzuli Freda

Erzuli Freda is one of the Erzuli family of Lwa in Dahomey and Haitian Voodoo traditions. She is depicted as the Mater Dolorosa or the Black Madonna in artworks, and, like Venus, is the ruler of love, beauty, jewellery, dancing, luxury and flowers. She wears three wedding rings – one for each of her husbands (Damballah, Agwe and Ogun) and her colours are pink, blue, white and gold. Offerings to her include jewellery, perfume, and sweet things. She is considered vain by some, flirty by others, and is associated with flirtation and seduction.

Ishtar

Ishtar was a Mesopotamian goddess of war and sexual love. She is also associated with Inanna (Sumerian) and Astarte (Semitic). She is associated with storehouses, and therefore dates, meat, grain, and wool. She is the goddess of rain and thunderstorms and is primarily known as a goddess of fertility. Ishtar is also associated with the planet Venus and is depicted in Sumerian reliefs as a bright star, forming a triad with Shamash (the sun) and Sin (the moon).

The Erotes

In the Greek Pantheon, Aphrodite is accompanied by an entourage of seven gods who are all associated with different aspects of love and lust. Anteros is the god of unrequited love, Eros the god of love and procreation, Himeros is the god of sexual desire, Hedylogos the god of sweet talk and flattery, Hermaphroditus (see Mercury), Hymen is the god of marriage and weddings, and Pothos the god of sexual yearning and desire.

Venusian Tarot

The Empress

The Empress can represent the archetype of the mother – the Mater Dolorosa. She represents the more benign aspects of the divine feminine – love, gentleness, and nourishment. She also signified sexuality, emotions, and the female as mistress of her own domain. She represents passions over ideas, emotions over intellect. Like her planetary ruler, she is creativity, beauty, and kindness, but she also has a great deal of spiritual strength. An accomplished woman with an appreciation of the arts, she is peace, prosperity and harmony. An admirable woman who is an inspirational role model, she adheres to her own values.

Practical Venusian Magic

An apple spell to bring love

Before we begin, it's worth noting that in the Western Mystery traditions we are taught to not name specific people in our love spells without consent, as it would be considered manipulation of a person's free will. As tempting as it can be when you are caught in the full force of an unrequited love, naming the person tends to result in a simple backfiring of the magic (you might get more obsessed, while to them you are simply invisible etc). Instead, focus on bringing in a more general calling for love – the perfect love for you.

On a Friday (or at the hour of Venus), take one apple and cut off the top. Using a teaspoon, hollow out the inside, making sure to retain the pips. Write your wish on some paper or parchment using green or pink ink, using the SMART formula we looked at in the first chapter. That means phrase it in the present tense, for example, 'It is July 2023, and I am out walking in the woods with my beloved'. Place the paper inside the apple with seven of any of the following: apple pips, rose petals, myrtle leaves, hibiscus flowers, a piece of rose quartz (or seven rose quartz chips).

Bury the apple in some soil, and let it work its magic. Do not return to see if it has grown but have faith that it has.

A Venusian Sacred Bath for Self-Love

A recipe for a purifying sacred bath: Salt is a deep cleanser on an energetic level, and Epsom salts are an old cure for aching muscles.

On a Friday (or at the hour of Venus) take one cup of sea salt and half a cup of Epsom salts. Mix them together, whilst picturing your soothing intent. Then add seven drops each of rose, geranium, and clary sage oils. Then count in 49 rose petals.

Mix well, add a cup full to a nice warm bath, and sit back and soak.

Venusian Tea

For this you will need either a good old-fashioned tea pot, a tea infuser, a tea strainer, or a packet of re-fillable tea bags. If you want to mix up a batch of this ahead of time, just increase the quantities in sevens, and then store it in an airtight jar away from direct sunlight.

Take:

7 rose petals

7 hibiscus petals

7 pinches of heather blossom

7 pieces of dried apple (you can hand dry this at home on a radiator, in a low oven or in a warm place. Don't use fresh – it will turn your tea mouldy in the jar!)

Add the herbs to your teapot or infuser, pour on boiled water, and leave it to steep for 7 minutes. While it is infusing, stir and picture Mercury's positive influence in your life.

Chapter 6

Creating Sun Magic

Hear golden Titan, whose eternal eye
With broad survey, illumines all the sky.
Self-born, unwearied in diffusing light,
And to all eyes the mirrour of delight:
Lord of the seasons, with thy fiery car
And leaping coursers, beaming light from far:
With thy right hand the source of morning light,
And with thy left the father of the night.
Agile and vig'rous, venerable Sun,
Fiery and bright around the heav'ns you run.
Foe to the wicked, but the good man's guide,
O'er all his steps propitious you preside:
With various founding, golden lyre, 'tis mine
To fill the world with harmony divine.
Father of ages, guide of prosp'rous deeds,
The world's commander, borne by lucid steeds,
Immortal Jove, all-searching, bearing light,
Source of existence, pure and fiery bright
Bearer of fruit, almighty lord of years,
Agil and warm, whom ev'ry pow'r reveres.
Great eye of Nature and the starry skies,
Doom'd with immortal flames to set and rise
Dispensing justice, lover of the stream,
The world's great despot, and o'er all supreme.
Faithful defender, and the eye of right,
Of steeds the ruler, and of life the light:
With founding whip four fiery steeds you guide,
When in the car of day you glorious ride.
Propitious on these mystic labours shine,

And bless thy suppliants with a life divine.
(Orphic Hymn VII to The Sun[11])

Introducing the Sun

A heading like that sounds faintly ridiculous, doesn't it? We are all well acquainted with the sun, or lack of it, depending on where you live. There shouldn't be many surprises in this chapter. The sun is associated with Mediterranean climates, right? And Mediterranean diets. Yes, absolutely, but this isn't a modern invention. It is also associated with all the good stuff – health, healing (think of all that vitamin D), and success. If you want an all-round boost of success and health energy, then the sun is the 'planet' for you.

Of course, we know it's not a planet, but the pre-moderns weren't aware of that fact. They also didn't realise that Earth and all the other planets in our solar system revolved around the sun. Remember, this was an earth-centric world view, which is why Earth doesn't appear in our planetary line-up. (For earth attributions, you will need to refer to elemental correspondences instead).

The sun, like the moon, is a body that people have written songs and poetry for since the beginning of humankind. If you want a lovely ritual to the sun, then consider going to a lovely, sun-bathed spot, and reading aloud Shakespeare's thirty-third sonnet:

Full many a glorious morning have I seen
Flatter the mountaintops with sovereign eye,
Kissing with golden face the meadows green,
Gilding pale streams with heavenly alchemy;
Anon permit the basest clouds to ride
With ugly rack on his celestial face
And from the forlorn world his visage hide,
Stealing unseen to west with this disgrace.

Even so my sun one early morn did shine
With all-triumphant splendour on my brow;
But out, alack! he was but one hour mine;
The region cloud hath mask'd him from me now.
Yet him for this my love no whit disdaineth;
Suns of the world may stain when heaven's sun staineth.[12]

Solar deities, however, might surprise you.

Working with Sol

Working with solar energies can encourage ideas of sovereignty – where are you a sovereign of your own realm? It can also bring with it healing energies, and health-some qualities, not just with regards to physical health, but also with mental and spiritual health as well. It is that ever illusive holistic health we all go in search of. Sol is also the planet you call on for help with achieving your ambitions and activating your solar plexus – the energy centre which wants to exercise its authority, and feel its way in the world. It brings with it wealth, and achievement borne of hard work, success, and talent, not just the brute force of Martian will or the trickster energy of Mercury.

Solar Symbols and Sigils

The solar glyph, taken from astrological and alchemical sources, is a simple circle with a dot in the middle.

Guido Bonatti's illustration shows the young king Sol being drawn in his chariot by horses, the wheel depicting his astrological sign, Leo. On his head, the crown of kinship, in his hand a stave. Around his head, like all good sun / son gods, his solar halo is visible.

Agrippa's Solar Magic

Agrippa's Kamea for the sun contains 6 rows and columns (giving us a principle number of 6 for the sun) giving us 36 numbers in total. The rows and columns each add up to 111, and the total of the Kamea is 666.

6	32	3	34	35	1
7	11	27	28	8	30
19	14	16	15	23	24
18	20	22	21	17	13
25	29	10	9	26	12
36	5	33	4	2	31

The seal of the sun is shown below.

Agrippa's Solar Suffumigation

According to Agrippa:

> *We make a suffumigation for the Sun in this manner, viz. of Saffron, Amber, Musk, Lignum-aloes, the fruit of the Laurell, Cloves, Myrrh, and Frankincense, all which being bruised, and mixt in such a proportion as may make a sweet odour, must be incorporated with the brain of an Eagle, or the blood of a white Cock, after the manner of pills, or Troches.* [8]

Thankfully, we do not need to make incenses using ingredients derived from animals today, however, it does give you a sense of what animals are under the dominion of Sol according to Agrippa – Eagles, and a white cockerel (I notice Cornelius doesn't recommend any lion parts in his recipe). His herbs include saffron, amber, musk, lignum aloes, as well as bay leaf, clove, myrrh and frankincense (in fact Agrippa also tells us that 'to the sun, gums, frankincense, mastic, benjamin, storax, ladanum, ambergris and musk').

Solar Incense

A cruelty-free incense to bring health, success, and general fulfilment. To burn an incense, you will need a censor – a heatproof container (either a metal thurible, or an old mug or earthenware dish). Fill it to 1cm below the top with earth, salt, or sand. You will also need some small charcoal. It is also useful to have a pestle and mortar for this, to grind the ingredients together.

You will need:

A dessert spoon of frankincense pearls
6 bay leaves (laurel)
1 teaspoon of marigold (calendula) petals (more affordable than Saffron, but feel free to substitute if you want to).
6 drops of orange essential oil
6 drops of neroli essential oil

On a Sunday, or at the hour of Sol, begin by grinding the dried flowers in a pestle and mortar, then add the resin, and finally the essential oils. As you mix, think about the success or healing that you want to encourage. You can even picture yourself lying in a sunlit spot, soaking up the sun's rays through your closed eyelids, or read aloud the Orphic Hymn to the Sun as you mix, and when you feel the energy within you reach a pinnacle, say the words, 'And so it is'.

Fill the censor with salt or sand and place a lit charcoal disc on top (you may also like to use tweezers or sugar tongs for handling the charcoal to prevent burns). When the charcoal starts to turn grey in colour, it is ready for use. Sprinkle on the incense, making sure you keep the windows open, and the room well aired. It's also best to keep your feathered and furred folk in another room.

As the incense smoke goes skyward, think about Sol's healing energies surrounding you.

Solar Deities

What can be confusing about Solar deities is that both the Sun and Jupiter (as planets) hold characteristics of kingship. The medieval woodcuts of the planets often show Sol as wearing a crown, and sometimes is accompanied by the Latin, Dei Praefectus (Chief God). However, while the Jupiterian deities tend to be the Father-god figures, the solar ones are often the Sun / Son gods. How you see the gods will be unique to you, and it is important to make up your own mind about what they are and who they are. My grandfather High Priest once told me that 'God was a concept created by humans to explain the unexplainable'. I interpret that as an indicator that (for me) deities are somewhat akin to archetypes, the theory put forward by Carl Jung to help us to understand the human experience across cultures and centuries. When we work with deities as archetypes, the Solar deities are the ones who are often the sacrificial gods – those gods who were wedded to the land and the people and sacrificed that the people might continue. You mind this view reductive, but it enables us to identify patterns and themes. Working with them as archetypes also means that their gender becomes less rigid. Our gods reflect us, and we reflect them. The Northern sun deity, Sól, is feminine.

Jesus, or the Sacrificial Sun / Son

It's hard to write a brief introductory paragraph to Jesus when so many people have grown up in Christian families. Even if you grew up in an agnostic setting, where church was somewhere you went on high days and holidays, or if you were brought up in an entirely different religion altogether, you will likely have opinions about who you think this deity is, because he is so prevalent across the world. We still live in a largely monotheistic-centric world view and coupled with our various other levels of privilege and illusions of superiority, it's hard to unpick Jesus as a deity without hitting a few hot-buttons for people. If this rankles for you, bear with me.

If I can ask you to park what you think you know about Jesus for a moment, and think in terms of archetypes, it's possible to then see some running themes through many of our solar deities. The use of the words 'Dei Praefectus', or chief god on the pre-modern woodcuts gives us a connection here. Gods that fall under the solar banner are also often depicted with a golden halo around their heads, which depicts their enlightenment or holiness. Think Jesus, Buddha, Mithras, Ra – all of them wear a solar disc, sometimes with solar rays, and sometimes golden in colour.

There are lots of theories on the internet that will tell you that Jesus, Horus, Mithras etc are all the same god-story retold across the ages. I will leave you to do your own research and make up your own mind on that one. There is, however, a case for them being similar in theme as archetypes of a sacrificial sun god, who dies for the good of their people, and (in some cases) is resurrected. Some of them have a miraculous birth (Osiris, Mithras), have baptism as a feature of their worship (Mithras, Jesus) and are celebrated using bread to represent their body and wine or ale to represent their blood (Jesus, Osiris, Mithras, Dionysus).

It might be too reductive to suggest they are the *same* gods recycled over time, but human societies do tend to have a fondness for stories with these themes, and he is an intriguing archetype to work with.

In my second-degree training, I had to choose an individual deity to spend a month with – learning about their stories, eating their foods, worshipping at their altar. I chose Jesus, and my overriding impression was how painful it was. I incurred many losses that month – a row of trees that I loved and spent many hours in the presence of were inexplicably cut down without warning, budget cuts at work that meant one of my team was let go (she's ok now – she took the opportunity to re-train as a lawyer). While none of it was majorly life-changing for me, it did make me think about the nature of sacrifice and remind me of how our sense of control in life is illusory.

Mithras

The cult of Mithras was a Roman mystery cult that centred on a deity whose origins were found in the Zoroastrian tradition. Worshippers of Mithras had a series of initiations they had to undertake, and the followers gathered in underground temples to worship Mithras. A Mithraeum was uncovered in London following the Blitz which is thought to date back to the year 240CE. Very little is known about the cult, since it was a mystery tradition, and no writings survived that described the rites. The cult of Mithras was eventually suppressed when Christianity became the dominant Roman religion.

Sol (Norse) or Sunna (Old High German)

Sól is a female solar deity who comes from Germanic mythology. She is mentioned in both the *Poetic Edda* and the *Prose Edda*, as the sister of the Moon god, Mani. *The Poetic Edda* recounts how Mani and his sister, Sól are pursued through the heavens by wolves. Sól seeks shelter in the protecting woods through the night, while Mani continues to be chased.

The Aten, Ra, and Ra-Horakhty

Ancient Egypt is one of the most fascinating periods of world history, but also one of the most deeply complex due to the length and breadth of the period we label as simply 'Ancient Egypt'. As a result, the deities of the Egyptian pantheon as equally as complex, and often morphed and changed over the (approximately) thirty centuries of this period that began with the unification of Egypt around 3100 BCE and ended with the invasion of Alexander the Great in 332 BCE.

Ra is one of the Ancient Egyptian deities who represents the

Sun God, but this group of gods also changed and morphed during the long history of Egypt, sometimes changing names or becoming conflated with other deities. The history of worship in Ancient Egypt is almost more interesting that the qualities of the individual solar god(s).

Ra was always seen as the father of the Pharoah, who was often represented by the god Horus. In common with other solar gods, Ra was the chief deity in the Pantheon and held esteem. However, the story of this Solar deity also touches on the story of the most famous Pharoah of them all – Tutankhamun – or more accurately, King Tut's (possible) father, Akhenaton (the jury is still out on that one). Akhenaten was the husband of Nefertiti and is most well-known for his attempts at introducing a new religion to Ancient Egypt – one that abandoned the polytheistic worship of many gods and centred on the worship of one solar god – the Aten. The cult grew in influence during Akhenaten's reign, but following his death, its popularity quickly fell away, and the people returned to their polytheistic religion of choice. When Tutankhamun was born, he was named Tutankhaten, but as his reign progressed and polytheism returned, the boy king's name was changed to distance him from Akhenaton and the diminishing monotheism.

Ra in his purest form is a much simpler depiction of a sun god – the principal deity and father figure of all creation who is frequently represented by the scarab beetle holding the sun's disc between its front legs. He is also depicted with the falcon head and wearing the sun's disc, which later became conflated with Horus. Ra-Horakhty, who is a combination of the two deities. The worship of Ra was eventually faded out as the Roman Empire introduced Christianity. Ra-Horakhty (which translates as 'Ra who is Horus of the Horizons') was a much later deity who brought in themes of the sun's journey from horizon point to horizon point, and is also symbolic of birth, death, and rebirth. There are some beautiful hymns to the

Egyptian gods that survived on temple walls.

Solar Tarot

The Sun

Under the sun, everything becomes simple, joyous, and physical. It represents the unconscious being brought out into the daylight. There is a childlike joy to the card that reminds us to be present, in the moment, and free ourselves of concerns about what might come tomorrow. In its daily journey across the sky, the sun sees everything, and so the card can also signify knowledge, clarity, and lucidity. They are, quite simply, filled with light. The universe is unified and alive, and the garden of Eden was never really lost – we were just looking in the wrong place by looking outside ourselves for perfection. The Sun card represents joy, happiness, and the beauty of life.

Strength

The Strength card can mark the beginning of the journey into the self, where the masks of the ego must fall away, allowing the seeker to find the true source of their inner strength. While the idea of the 'death of the ego' is somewhat reductive – a little ego is essential for some things – the idea of finding and tapping into your own inner source of strength is a crucial part of the Fool's Journey from birth to enlightenment. (By the way, if you haven't sussed it yet, we are all the Fool in this journey!) The Strength card can indicate the need to have the courage and strength to achieve your own goals, and it can mean the need for ambition tempered with a little humility. We must have the courage of our convictions, and the discipline to channel our energy towards the one goal. It can also indicate the taming of the ego and understanding the consequences of our actions.

Practical Solar Magic

A Solar Oil for Success

This recipe can be used for anointing yourself, your magical tools or solar crystals, or your candles in candle magic (see the spell below).

On a Sunday, gather 6 golden dandelion heads in good sunlight. Make sure you gather ecologically (leave enough for the bees) and away from where dogs may have been. Steep them in half a cup of olive or sunflower oil for 24 hours – leave it on a warm windowsill to get maximum sunshine for 24 hours, and then move it to somewhere dark and cool and leave it for a further six days (a week in total).

On the next Sunday, remove the dandelion heads and compost them. To the oil, add:

6 drops of orange essential oil
6 pieces of dried orange peel (you can dry this yourself at home on a radiator or in a warm spot, or buy it from an herbalist)
A piece of citrine or yellow calcite
Six drops of frankincense essential oil (or six frankincense tears if you prefer to use the resin)

As you mix, visualise the successful outcome you are working for – the job offer letter, the house purchase, recovery from an illness, whatever endeavour you need a dose of solar success for. Then use it to anoint you, the item you want to bring a successful result in, or to anoint a candle for a candle spell (see below!)

A Solar Salve

To make a solar salve (which you can use as a lip salve or a balm) then make up the recipe as if for the solar oil but add two tablespoons of melted beeswax.

First, warm the oil in a double boiler (or zap it for fifteen seconds in a microwave). To make a makeshift double boiler, you can use a Pyrex jug in a pot with about three centimetres of simmering water.

When the oil is warm (not hot!) add the beeswax and stir the mixture until the beeswax has completely melted. Then pour it into a tin or a jar and allow the mixture to set. Do use recycled pots and tins wherever possible. One of my favourite gifts last year was a pot of salve a friend had made in a recycled mints tin.

A Solar Candle for Health
You will need:

A gold or yellow candle (a 'spell candle' will burn for an hour or two, a dinner sized candle will last a full seven hours, so you might like to invest in some spell candles of mixed colours. I keep a selection of all seven colours in the house, so I have always got one to hand).
A cocktail stick, a pencil or something pointy for carving the candle
6 drops of the solar oil we made previously

On a Sunday, take your candle, and carve the solar glyph and your initials (or the initials of the person who has requested the healing spell) onto the candle, and then anoint it with six drops of your solar oil, all the while stating your intended outcome in the present tense (for example, 'it is January 20th and I am feeling fit and healthy' Better still, visualise yourself doing something you associate with health – walking in the local park, or even cooking yourself a healthy meal. However small it might seem, it doesn't matter. Really focus on how it feels to be doing that thing.

If you struggle with visualisation, try to imagine on what

you will see, hear, taste, smell and feel when you get the result. When you have that vision really clear in your mind's eye, or that feeling in your body, visualise all of that going into the candle, then light it, and end with a 'And so it is'.

Chapter 7

Creating Mars Magic

Magnanimous, unconquer'd, boistrous Mars,
In darts rejoicing, and in bloody wars
Fierce and untam'd, whose mighty pow'r can make
The strongest walls from their foundations shake:
Mortal destroying king, defil'd with gore,
Pleas'd with war's dreadful and tumultuous roar:
Thee, human blood, and swords, and spears delight,
And the dire ruin of mad savage fight.
Stay, furious contests, and avenging strife,
Whose works with woe, embitter human life;[10]
To lovely Venus, and to Bacchus yield,
To Ceres give the weapons of the field;
Encourage peace, to gentle works inclin'd,
And give abundance, with benignant mind.
(Orphic Hymn LXIV to Mars[13])

Introducing Mars

Mars is one of the most challenging of the planets to understand, as it is often labelled with qualities that we might struggle to integrate – brute force, strength, and masculinity. When I teach Mars workshops, I often ask my students to consider the way in which Mars can represent toxic masculinity and the Patriarchy at its binary worst, but it can also offer us the opportunity to explore a healthier masculinity, one which is better for all genders, including the male. It also gives us the opportunity to explore the feminine archetypes associated with these apparently masculine traits.

Mars is often paired with Venus as the divine feminine

and the divine masculine together, and in the Renaissance period particularly, Mars was often depicted alongside his lover Venus. Think Sandro Botticelli's Mars and Venus – the portrait that suggests Mars could only relax when Venus had 'tamed' him, post-coitus. In this depiction he is the God of War who stamps his will through brute force, however, the planet Mars is more subtle than that. There is also a softer side to it, one where it is the planet associated with gardening and agriculture, which often takes people by surprise. There was a practical reason for this – in our distant past as a largely agricultural species, war called upon farmers to become foot soldiers. When it was time for the crops to be gathered, all wars had to be paused to allow the soldier-farmers to return, and for the harvest to be brought home. This was crucial in avoiding widespread winter starvation.

Guido Bonatti's Mars from the *Book of Heavenly Influences* shows him riding into battle on his chariot, drawn by war horses, holding his sword and shield, and wearing his armour. The wheels of his chariot depict his astrological signs, Aries and Scorpio (which is ruled by Pluto in modern astrology).

Mars also reminds me of my paternal grandfather – a very gentle man who spent many years away from home during the Second World War. He was conscripted into the army and had to travel overseas. When he returned seven years later, he wanted nothing more than to spend quiet time in his garden, growing his favourite roses. I am sure his experience of war was like that of thousands of his generation, and beyond.

Working with Mars

Mars is a very helpful energy to call on if you are ever in the position of needing to be more assertive and exercise your boundaries. If you struggle with defending your own space (energetic or physical) then Mars can help you to say, 'No, and no further', a response we all need to be able to use at times to avoid being completely overwhelmed by other people. At its most healthy, think assertiveness classes, and the stubbornness that is sometimes needed to keep chipping away at a task until it is done. At the opposite end of the spectrum, we get the negative, more toxic side – stubborn to the point of belligerence, quick to anger, and enough fire to scorch anyone who comes too close. But then, who doesn't love a little bit of a fire to keep us warm on the cold nights?

Martian Symbols and Sigils

The classical alchemical and astrological Mars glyph is also the symbol for masculinity and is formed from the shield and spear or sword of the god himself.

Agrippa's Martian Magic

Agrippa's kamea gives us a magical number square which has 5 rows and columns, giving us a principle number of 5 for Mars. The kamea has 25 numbers in total. Each row, column or diagonal adds up to 65, and the square adds up to 325 in total.

11	24	7	20	3
4	12	25	8	16
17	5	13	21	9
10	18	1	14	22
23	6	19	2	15

The kamea then generates the following Seal of Mars:

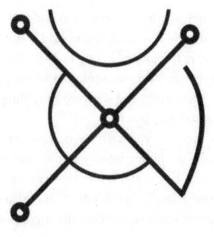

Agrippa's Mars Suffumigation

Agrippa tells us in *The Book of Natural Magic*, that 'to Mars, all odiferous wood, such as sanders, cypress, lignum balsam and lignum aloes.' For a suffumigation, he suggests,

> *For Mars, take euphorbium, bedellium, gum ammoniac, the roots of both hellebores, the loadstones, and a little sulphur; and incorporate them all with the brain of a hart, the blood of a man and the blood of a black cat.*[8]

This tells us that Agrippa's animals include the black cat, the hart, and the human male. The stones include lodestones, and the herbs include euphorbium, hellebore root, and gum ammoniac. Cypress is sometimes attributed to Saturn (as cypress trees tend to be grown in cemeteries in the Mediterranean). Not only would this ingredient list including animal parts be cruel, but it would also be incredibly ponky. Sulphur smells appalling when you burn it. To avoid all the ethical dilemmas and the stink, I would recommend using a more modern take on herbal correspondences with my own recipe below.

A Martian Incense for Asserting Your Boundaries around a Space

I once had an incident in an incense making workshop where my Mars table decided to wing it and add some dried chilli to their Mars incense. It was a perfectly logical thing to do since it is a Martian herb, however, we soon had to evacuate the room, as our eyes were watering, and we were coughing so hard. Some herbs are best eaten, not burned.

To burn an incense, you will need a censor – a heatproof container (either a metal thurible, or an old mug or earthenware dish). Fill it to 1cm below the top with earth, salt, or sand. You will also need some small charcoal discs. It is also useful to have a pestle and mortar for this, to grind the ingredients together.

You will need:

Five teaspoons of frankincense pearls
Five pinches of dragon's blood resin
A small pinch of black peppercorns (crushed up finely)
Five pine needles (cut up into small pieces)
5 drops of black pepper essential oil
5 drops of pine essential oil

On a Tuesday, or at the hour of Mars, begin by grinding the dried peppercorns in a pestle and mortar, then add the resin, and finally the essential oils. As you mix, think about the boundary that you want to hold firm to. You can read aloud the Orphic Hymn to Ares as you mix, and when you feel the energy within you reach a pinnacle, say the words, 'And so it is'.

Fill the censor with salt or sand and place a lit charcoal disc on top (you may also like to use tweezers or sugar tongs for handling the charcoal to prevent burns). When the charcoal starts to turn grey in colour, it is ready for use. Sprinkle on the incense, making sure you keep the windows open, and the room well aired. It's also best to keep your feathered and furred folk in another room.

As the incense smoke goes skyward, think about Mars's energies surrounding you.

Martian Deities

Mars's cousins and counterparts are usually the warrior deities. Aside from Ogun, the ones I am choosing to share here are feminine deities. Although that was not necessarily a conscious decision, it's very Martian to overturn a few ingrained beliefs. Each of the deities is associated with a fiery passion and a temper to match, but is also important to recognise that, even our ancient ancestors knew that while these qualities might be challenging, suppressing them can be very unhealthy. If you are struggling with these aspects of yourself, work towards integrating those passions, acknowledging where they help you to push through and get tasks done, instead of berating yourself, repressing the emotion and making yourself ill.

Pele

In indigenous Hawaiian traditions, Pele is the goddess of volcanoes and fire. Known as Pele of the Sacred Land, she descended from the earth mother and the sky father. Pele is one of the fire sisters who inhabits the volcano Kilauea, where she inhabits a fire pit, but she encompasses all volcanic activity on the island.

She is said to be able to change form, becoming variously a dog, an old woman, or a beautiful young woman who comes to warn the islanders about impending eruptions. She is also significant in the practice of hula dancing, and has many dances dedicated to her. While she is known for her capriciousness, her fiery temper, and her jealousy, she is also the goddess who created the islands.

Kali

Kali could equally have been placed amongst the line-up of Saturnian deities, as she is the Hindu goddess associated with time, change, and death, which puts her very firmly in alignment with Saturn. However controversially, I am placing her within the Martian line-up due to the fact she is known for having a voracious bloodlust that only Sekhmet would have been able to relate to. Her name in Sanskrit means 'the fullness of time', and she is the female counterpart of Lord Shiva. One of her most well-known stories is that of her appearance on the battlefield (which again links her with Mars energy) where she is depicted as having eyes that are red with rage and intoxication, while she stands on corpses and rips their heads off.

However, despite her apparent gruesomeness, Kali is a much-loved goddess associated with destroying evil to protect the innocent, so she is a divine protectress and a liberator. She is also associated with mother nature and is the preserver of nature.

Sekhmet

In the Egyptian religions, Sekhmet, the lion-headed goddess, was associated with being the destroyer of the sun god, Ra. She led pharaohs onto the battlefield, where she lives up to her names – 'She who is Mighty', 'The One Before Whom Evil Trembles', 'Mistress of Dread', and 'She who Mauls'. Her most famous story relates how Ra sends Sekhmet out amongst the people to destroy those who conspired against him; however, she becomes so enraged with bloodlust, that she will not stop killing. In the end, Ra had to trick her into drinking beer that had been died red, so that she became intoxicated and slept.

She is depicted as a woman with a lion's head, and she wears the divine Solar disc and the Uraeus (the cobra crown).

Ogun

Ogun is one of the Orishas in the Yoruban religion (from Nigeria). He is a god of war, politics, metals, and the traditional deity of warriors, hunters, and blacksmiths. His primary symbols are iron, a palm frond and a dog. He also features in Candomblé traditions as Ogum, in Santeria as Ogun, and in Haitian Vodou as Ogou. Often depicted holding a machete, traditional offerings to Ogun include rum poured on the ground (which is then set alight), and tobacco.

Martian Tarot

The Emperor

The Emperor can be a tricky card to integrate, particularly in a world that is still overwhelmingly patriarchal, which is not good for any gender. The Feminine and Gender Fluid are oppressed, while the Masculine is put under pressure to be something it cannot be without cost to itself. At its worst the Emperor card can represent toxic masculinity, just as its ruler Mars can. At its best, it can be tempered with humility, the willingness to listen and learn, and use its power wisely. In this overwhelmingly patriarchal worldview that gave birth to the archetypes of the Tarot, the Emperor bears the authority, the ability to sit in judgement, and dictate the laws of society. The card can represent the Father, Husband, Ruler (the capital letters are there for a reason, as I am referring to the archetypes here). He can also be a figure that is remote, emotionally absent, and quite cold. In ancient times, the Goddess ruled the world, while the King performed a sacred function in being wedded to the land in the Hieros Gamos, or Great Rite, before being sacrificed in winter to fertilise the land.

At its best, the Emperor represents wisdom and power, a mature man of distinction, or a caring person with many responsibilities. It can also indicate the need to rise to meet a challenge, impressive leadership in the face of fear and uncertainty, and reason ruling over emotion.

The Tower

A bit like the Death card, people often fear the Tower. It can signify a period of chaos where the illusion of control has been struck by lightning and burned to the ground. It also represents unheeded warnings – likely this situation has arisen because you didn't pay attention to the warning signs which were flashing like lighthouses in the darkness. You have lived under a false sense of security, and something has come to strip away all illusions, and raze your tower to the ground. However, this gives a unique opportunity to begin again, to rebuild the tower with better foundations. The destruction of the old ways gives the opportunity for new growth and renewal.

When I first started studying tarot, my teacher encouraged us to learn the major arcana by carrying them with us for a week as homework. We would then begin each class with a debrief as to what had happened that week. Pity us poor students – his method for the 'big bad three' was to ask us to carry round the Tower, Death, and the Devil in the same week so we could limit the trail of destruction to one week only.

Practical Martian Magic

Practical Mars magic will usually involve a component of fire since that is its element. If you want to invoke Mars in your life, its best to always keep it supervised, but practical magic doesn't always have to involve formal spells. Why not build an altar to Mars in your living space? You can use a red altar cloth, red candles, a representation of the glyph – either on parchment, or by making a sigil using the craft-clay that you bake in the oven. You can use altar time to evoke Mars with poems, to remind it that you are working together on a particular project. You can also wear red clothes or carry red crystals as reminder.

Mars Oil

This recipe can be used for anointing yourself, your magical tools or Mars crystals, or your candles in candle magic (see the spell below). On a Tuesday, mix:

> 5 drops of Petitgrain oil
> 5 drops ginger essential oil
> 5 drops black pepper oil
> Half a cup of any pure base oil (for example, almond, olive oil or coconut oil, not a hydrogenated oil that has been processed).
> A piece of red jasper

As you mix, visualise the successful outcome you are working for – courage, assertiveness, passion, sex, whatever endeavour you need a dose of Mars success for. Then use it to anoint you, the item you want to bring a successful result in, or to anoint a candle for a candle spell (see below!)

A Mars Candle for Creativity
You will need:

A red candle
A cocktail stick, a pencil or something pointy for carving the candle
6 drops of the Mars oil we made previously

On a Tuesday, take your candle, and carve the Mars glyph and your initials onto the candle, and then anoint it with 5 drops of your Mars oil, all the while stating your intended outcome in the present tense (for example, 'it is January 20th, and I am busy painting / writing my book / making jewellery.' Better still, visualise yourself doing your chosen creative act. However small it might seem, it doesn't matter. Really focus on how it feels to be doing that thing. If you struggle with visualisation, try to imagine on what you will see, hear, taste, smell and feel when you get the result. When you have that vision really clear in your mind's eye, or that feeling in your body, visualise all of that going into the candle, then light it, and end with a 'And so it is'.

A Martian spell for the end of the affair
Mars can be helpful for asserting boundaries, as I have previously mentioned, but you can also use its fiery nature to send things away. To do this, you will need a heatproof container, and I would recommend you do this outside if you don't live in a home with a fireplace or wood burner. If you are burning things, there is always a lot more ash than you would anticipate. You might think there is little magic involved in this – it's a ceremony people have been doing following breakups for generations – but on a magical level it is useful for drawing

a line under something and energetically closing a door. You are not intending harm to the person; you are giving yourself closure on the relationship. Once performed, it is important that you move on. Don't speak ill of the person, and don't be tempted to go back and pick at the scab again. Go get yourself a good counsellor, a new hairstyle, a new outlook, and move on.

You will need:

A heatproof container (Cast iron cauldrons work well for this if you don't have a fireplace)
All the mementos you have of the relationship – letters, photos etc
A lighter
Something like a candle in a hurricane glass that will stay lit even with a breeze

Take yourself somewhere outdoors and quiet, where you won't be disturbed. Sit quietly and think about the task in hand, and really take a moment to mindfully acknowledge what you are feeling. It might be sadness; it might be anger. Whatever it is, don't judge the feeling, just acknowledge it, and honour it. Take a moment to think about the lessons this relationship has brought you. Has it taught you to be independent? To go on with a task regardless of the opposition you face? If you can extract the learning and acknowledge any kernel of good it brought you (even if it was simply that it showed you who really cared about you, and who was there with you to pick up the pieces when it all went wrong) then nothing is wasted. At the end of a particularly difficult relationship I had, what I was left with was my closest friends who had stood by me through a decade of difficulty, and this was my diamond in the rough that has stayed steady and constant ever since).

Set light to each item in turn, and as you do so, really release the person with love. If you need to, then petition Mars to extend his protective powers around you.

Chapter 8

Creating Jupiter Magic

O Jove, much-honour'd, Jove supremely great,
To thee our holy rites we consecrate,
Our pray'rs and expiations, king divine,
For all things to produce with ease thro' mind is thine.
Hence mother Earth and mountains swelling high
Proceed from thee, the deep and all within the sky.
Saturnian king, descending from above,
Magnanimous, commanding, sceptred Jove;
All-parent, principle and end of all,
Whose pow'r almighty shakes this earthly ball;
Ev'n Nature trembles at thy mighty nod,
Loud-sounding, arm'd with light'ning, thund'ring God.
Source of abundance, purifying king,
O various-form'd, from whom all natures spring;
Propitious hear my pray'r, give blameless health,
With peace divine, and necessary wealth.
(Orphic Hymn XIV to Jupiter[14])

Introducing Jupiter

Jupiter is the most benevolent of the planets, and is therefore a popular energy to call on, and a useful friend to have in life. While he is not the only planet to be associated with wealth (Mercury is the planet of bankers, and Sol is the planet of success), Jupiter tends to be a more stable long-lasting experience of wealth, comfort, choice, and enlargement. While Mercury might be a sudden windfall, and Sol might be a successful endeavour, Jupiter is property ownership, long-lasting investments, and the choice that comes from financial stability.

While some of the planets have a down-side that you need

to beware of (Mercury will take your money as fast as he gave it, Sol can bring a sense of false pride, Venus can be conceited) the main downside you might need to watch out for with Jupiter is an expanding waistline, overspending and excess.

Working with Jupiter

We work with Jupiter when we need to engender some expansion in our lives. It represents wealth, comfort, the sense of enlargement and success that tends to come in middle age. Jupiter's wealth tends to be more stable, and long lasting. It also brings harmonious energies to bear and is a useful ally if you are facing a legal battle of some kind. It is associated with benevolence, so it's also important to remember to give back if it bestows its blessings on you. Don't just hoard what you have been given – give to charity and pay it forward in the spirit of the planet itself.

Jupiterian Symbols and Sigils

Jupiter's Glyph looks a lot like a number 4, but it is a hieroglyph of an eagle, Jove's bird.

♃

This is echoed in Guido Bonatti's figure of Jupiter from 1297. He depicts Jupiter in a chariot drawn by eagles, bestowing his blessings on the figure of a boy or man, as he wears his crown and holds the sceptre of kingship. His wheels show his astrological signs – Sagittarius and Pisces (which is ruled by Neptune in modern astrology).

Agrippa's Jupiterian Magic

Agrippa's Kamea shows a square with 4 rows and columns, each adding up to 34. There are 16 numbers in total, and the number square adds up to 136. These are the numbers that can help you evoke Jupiter – you might choose to run a candle spell over 4 nights, using four purple candles, each anointed with 4 drops of oil.

4	14	15	1
9	7	6	12
5	11	10	8
16	2	3	13

The seal of Jupiter is also a useful sigil to be aware of. You may encounter it in grimoires, or on Jupiterian talismans.

Agrippa's Jupiter Suffumigation

Agrippa tells us that all 'odiferous fruits, as nutmegs and cloves' fall under Jupiter's dominion. For a suffumigation, he says,

> *For Jupiter, take the seed of ash, lignum aloes, storax, the gum benjamin or benzoin, the lazuli stone, and the tops of the feathers of a peacock; and incorporate them with the blood of a stork, or a swallow, or the brain of a hart.* [8]

Here, Agrippa gives us clues about the animals (stork, swallow, peacock, hart) of Jupiter, the herbs (ash, lignum aloes, storax, benzoin) as well as the crystals (lapis lazuli) to use in invoking Jupiter. As we are not in the business of using animal parts here, you could try my alternative.

A Jupiter Incense for Expansion and Wealth

To burn an incense, you will need a censor – a heatproof container (either a metal thurible, or an old mug or earthenware dish). Fill it to 1cm below the top with earth, salt, or sand. You will also need some small charcoal discs – the type used in shisha pipes, so you will find these in a local international supermarket, or online. It is also useful to have a pestle and mortar for this, to grind the ingredients together.

You will need:

4 teaspoons of frankincense pearls
4 pinches of benzoin resin (if it is in powdered form, or 4 small pieces if it is whole)
4 cloves (crushed up finely)
4 pieces of mace (crushed or cut up into small pieces)
4 drops of clove essential oil
4 drops of violet essential oil

On a Thursday, or at the hour of Jupiter, begin by grinding the dried mace and cloves in a pestle and mortar, then add the resins, and finally the essential oils. As you mix, think about the expansion that you want to experience. You can read aloud the Orphic Hymn to Jupiter as you mix, and when you feel the energy within you reach a pinnacle, say the words, 'So mote it be', or, 'and so it is'.

Fill the censor with salt or sand and place a lit charcoal disc on top (you may also like to use tweezers or sugar tongs for handling the charcoal to prevent burns). When the charcoal starts to turn grey in colour, it is ready for use. Sprinkle on the incense, making sure you keep the windows open, and the room well aired. It's also best to keep your feathered and furred folk in another room.

As the incense smoke goes skyward, think about Jupiter's energies surrounding you.

Jupiterian Deities

While the solar gods tended to be the son-gods, Jupiter's cousins and counterparts are all about the All-Father (a sky-related father figure). However, I have also included a feminine counterpart.

Odin

Odin is the much-loved patriarch of the Norse pantheon. Odin could equally be placed in the Saturnian section of this book (he is often depicted as an older man with one eye, and is associated with death and the gallows), he could also be associated with Mercury (his name is Woden in old English, which is the root of the name Wednesday) but I have him here as a cousin of Jupiter because of his association as the All-Father. He is the father of Thor and Baldr and is accompanied by his animal familiars a pair of wolves, as well as two ravens.

He is associated with wisdom, and healing, and in some texts, is depicted as the enthroned ruler of the gods, as well as the ancestral source of royalty. One of Odin's most well-known stories is that of his quest for wisdom. He hung himself upside down from the Yggdrasil (the tree of life) to gain insight (the origin of the Hanged Man tarot card). When he returned, he brought with him the runes, but had lost an eye in the process. He is also the deity associated with poetry, magic, and the Wild Hunt – a folkloric theme that takes him across the sea to the British Isles (most notably Dartmoor and Shropshire).

Damballah (or Danbala in Haiti)

Damballah is one of the most important of the Lwa, the spirits in the Vodou traditions of Haiti, Louisiana, and in other African diasporic religions. He is associated with being the Sky Father, using the coils of his serpent body to create the land and the stars. He is seen as being benevolent, patient, wise and kind. His presence is one that inspires peace, and he is considered the essence of purity. Offerings to him include an egg white placed on a mound of white flour, milk, white rice, and coconut.

Zeus

Zeus is the Greek counterpart to Jupiter, and pre-dates the Roman god. He is King of the Olympian gods, the husband of Hera, and father of Ares and Hephaestus. According to Homer's *The Iliad*, he also fathered Aphrodite. As a bit of a romantic philanderer, Zeus also fathered Athena, Apollo, Hermes, Persephone, Dionysus, Perseus, Heracles, Helen of Troy, Minos, and the Muses. Like Odin he is an All-father and his symbols include the thunderbolt, an eagle, a bull, and an oak tree.

His father was Cronos (Saturn's Greek counterpart), the leader of the Titans (the Pantheon that pre-dated the Olympians). Cronos was told that he would be deposed by his son, so each time a child was born (Hestia, Demeter, Hera, Hades, and Poseidon) he swallowed them. To prevent Zeus from suffering the same fate, his mother Rhea presented Cronos with a boulder wrapped in blankets, which he promptly swallowed, and hid Zeus away in Crete. When Zeus grew to adulthood, he went back to Cronos and forced him to disgorge the boulder, and then his other siblings. Zeus then overthrew Cronos and the other Titans and ruled from Mount Olympus.

Juno

Juno is Jupiter's feminine counterpart, and the chief goddess of the Roman religion. In the Greek pantheon, her equivalent would have been Hera. She related to the lives of women, in all their aspects, not just as the goddess of marriage, childbirth, and the female principle of life. As her popularity spread, Juno became the saviour of the state. She was associated with geese, the wild fig tree, and her festival – the Matronalia – was held on July 7th. Sometimes she is presented in military regalia.

Jupiterian Tarot

The Wheel of Fortune

The Wheel of Fortune is summed up in one simple statement for me – 'this too shall pass', because it refers to the good and the ill. All things move and shift, and the only thing certain in this life is change. Like the great Wheel of the Year or the karmic wheel, the Wheel of Fortune reminds us that time does not stay still – kings and the 'lucky' few may rise to fame, but they will also fall. It is as inevitable. It is a warning against pride, and it is also indicative of the end of a cycle, and the beginning of another. There might be a chance coming for wisdom and knowledge, for expansion and success, but there is also a need to recognise the window of opportunity is only temporary.

Temperance

Temperance is also a card that falls under the dominion of Jupiter. It indicates the ability to blend two opposing forces into something new – fire with water, spontaneity with knowledge. The word 'temperance' comes from the Latin 'temperare' which means to combine or mix properly. When it comes up in a reading, it indicates the ability to mix opposites and expand into something new. It is also indicative of the Greek goddess Iris, who travelled across the river Styx to the Underworld, and filled her golden cup from the river. The allegory implies that the blending of life's energies can only be achieved following the death of the ego.

Practical Jupiterian Magic

Jupiter Oil
This recipe can be used for anointing yourself, your magical tools or Jupiterian crystals, or your candles in candle magic (see the spell below). On a Thursday, mix:

  4 drops of clove oil
  4 drops oakmoss essential oil
  4 drops violet oil
  Half a cup of any pure base oil (for example, almond, olive oil or coconut oil, not a hydrogenated oil that has been processed).
  A piece of amethyst

As you mix, visualise Jupiter's influence in your life – wealth, expansion, comfort, a positive legal outcome you are working for, whatever endeavour you need a dose of Jupiterian success for. Then use the oil to anoint you, the item you want to bring a successful result in, or to anoint a candle for a candle spell (see below).

A Jupiter Candle for a Successful Legal Outcome
You will need:

  4 purple or royal blue candles
  A cocktail stick, a pencil or something pointy for carving the candle
  16 drops of the Jupiter oil we made previously

On a Thursday, take your candles, and carve the Jupiter glyph or seal onto the candle, along with your initials and the date of the legal case, then anoint each one with 4 drops of your Jupiter oil, all the while stating your intended outcome in the present tense (for example, 'it is January 20th and I have just been granted a positive outcome in court'). Better still, visualise yourself walking out of the court with a feeling of triumph. Really focus on how it feels. If you struggle with visualisation, try to name what you will see, hear, taste, smell and feel when you get the result. When you have that vision really clear in your mind's eye, or that feeling in your body, visualise all of that going into the candles, and end with a 'And so it is'. Light the first candle on the first Thursday at the hour of Jupiter (it will be just after dawn or check online for the up-to-date planetary hours that day). Then the following Thursday, light the second candle, on the third Thursday the third candle, and on the fourth Thursday, the final candle. If your need is desperate and you don't have four weeks, then you can switch to four subsequent days at the hour of Jupiter.

Jupiterian Tea

For this you will need either a good old-fashioned tea pot, a tea infuser, a tea strainer, or a packet of re-fillable tea bags (otherwise you will be chewing your tea, which is never a good look). Take:

4 cloves
A pinch or nutmeg (if it is powdered). If it is whole, crush it in a pestle and mortar and take 4 small pieces
4 borage flowers (you can buy this in International/Arabic supermarkets if you live in a city)
4 Sage leaves

Add the herbs to your teapot or infuser, pour on boiled water, and leave it to steep for 4 minutes. While it is infusing, stir and picture Jupiter's positive influence in your life.

Chapter 9

Creating Saturn Magic

Ethereal father, mighty Titan, hear,
Great fire of Gods and men, whom all revere:
Endu'd with various council, pure and strong,
To whom perfection and decrease belong.
Consum'd by thee all forms that hourly die,
By thee restor'd, their former place supply;
The world immense in everlasting chains, \
Strong and ineffable thy pow'r contains
Father of vast eternity, divine,
O mighty Saturn, various speech is thine:
Blossom of earth and of the starry skies,
Husband of Rhea, and Prometheus wife.
Obstetric Nature, venerable root,
From which the various forms of being shoot;
No parts peculiar can thy pow'r enclose,
Diffus'd thro' all, from which the world arose,
O, best of beings, of a subtle mind,
Propitious hear to holy pray'rs inclin'd;
The sacred rites benevolent attend,
And grant a blameless life, a blessed end.
(Orphic Hymn XII to Saturn[15])

Introducing Saturn

Saturn is probably the most feared and misunderstood of all the planets. As the slowest moving planet in our line-up, its effects are often the longest lasting. It is often depicted as an old man with a crutch, or sometimes as an amputee. It represents the darkest secrets that you uncover on an inward journey. There's a quote that has been attributed to the great Joseph Campbell, which says that 'The cave you fear to enter holds the treasure you seek.' This really encompasses everything that you will discover in your journey with Saturn.

Its most infamous act is that of our astrological Saturn Return, which relates to the point in your life during which Saturn returns to the place it was in your chart at your moment of birth. Saturn's orbit lasts around 28 to 30 years. This means, that we first encounter the Saturn Return when we reach the end of our 20s, and then again at the end of our 50s. This period can bring some challenges. Because Saturn is the ruler of stability, home, and your embodied sense of self, when Saturn returns to your birth chart, you start questioning everything you thought you knew about your life.

When I reached my first Saturn Return, it was the point at which I decided that everything I had been working towards through my teen years and my 20s was not what I had hoped it would be. It was at this time I went in search of a spiritual life and began my training as a witch. The reason I share this is that I hope you'll see that while you're going through your Saturn Return, the world can feel like a scary place, but often it brings necessary changes that help you to get to a better position in life.

Part of the fear of Saturn, is that it also rules endings, and sometimes endings can be a good thing. Its tarot card, not unsurprisingly, is the death card. It always represents the ending of a state, but that gives rise to the beginning of another.

Working with Saturn

Clearly, if you need to bring an ending to something, then Saturn is your planet. However, there is also another way in which Saturn can bring positive qualities to your life. It brings stability, grounding, and a level of protection. Banishing spells are Saturn's speciality, and I don't just mean banishing people – it can also help with banishing bad habits and self-destructive behaviours, and anything that is generally on helpful in your life. Saturn draws the line in the sand that says, 'no', 'I will go no further', and that is enough'. These are important phrases to have in your armoury.

Agrippa tells us Saturn rules places that are dark, underground caves. They tend to be places that smell deathly. That might sound grim, but I would add to this that they include the woods in winter, when the leaves have fallen from the trees and are lying underfoot, when they start to break down and you get that mulchy, earthy smell. When I used to live in London, I also used to joke that it was like the Underground in rush-hour, but truly, Saturn has a cold, damp feel. Each morning I walk along a nature trail which follows the line of a disused railway. Part of the trail leads through an old railway tunnel. It's invariably dark, running with water, and sounds are magnified to an echo. It has the feeling of a liminal space, one in which you pass between the worlds. This is Saturn in his essence. Part of you might be looking over your shoulder in fear for what's behind you, but there's also a safety in darkness, and a depth of intensity which is transformative. When you stand on the abyss and gaze into the very darkest depths of your soul, there are riches to be found there.

Saturnian Herb Craft

Saturn is one of the planets that comes with a very big health warning. When I teach incense making classes, I often set up the room with a table representing each planet. I find it interesting to see where people (unconsciously) choose to sit. It often represents an area they have a strength in, sometimes it's an area they need to work on. On each table I place bowls of different herbs, and bottles of essential oil that are ruled by that planet. The Saturn table is quite sparse. It has a black cloth, and only one or two herbs and essential oils – for example, patchouli, or vetiver oil. The reason for this is that most of the herbs ruled by Saturn are poisonous. When you look down the list of herbs and plants in the correspondence table at the end of this chapter, you will notice that many of them are hard to come by, and that's for a reason.

Food is a slightly easier to identify because we include root vegetables, and things that grow under the earth.

Saturnian Symbols and Sigils

Guido Bonnati's woodcut gives us an indication of some of Saturn's symbols. He is depicted riding in a chariot with his astrological signs – Capricorn and Aquarius – on the wheels. (Aquarius is ruled by Uranus in Modern Astrology). He holds a scythe in his hand, indicating that he is the reaper.

Saturn's astrological and alchemical glyph depicts a scythe or sickle.

$$\hbar$$

Agrippa's Saturnian Magic

Agrippa's Kamea for Saturn is short and sweet. It contains 3 rows and columns (indicating that 3 is Saturn's principle number). There are 9 numbers in total, with each row, column and diagonal adding up to 15. The total sum of the Kamea is 45.

4	9	2
3	5	7
8	1	6

Agrippa's seal of Saturn can be used to evoke the power of Saturn in candle spells and magical pouches, it can be written on the body, traced in the earth, written in herbs or salt or black chalk on the ground where you are working. There are any number of ways you can use it to call upon the energy of Saturn.

Agrippa's Suffumigation for Saturn

Agrippa writes that all 'odiferous roots' fall under Saturn – pepper-wort root, and the roots of the frankincense tree. For his suffumigation he suggests,

> For Saturn, take black poppy seed, henbane, root of mandrake, the loadstone, and myrrh, and make them up with the brain of a cat or the blood of a bat.[8]

As with the other planets, this reveals something of the stones, plants, and animals Agrippa links to Saturn's authority. Cats, bats, mandrake, henbane, black poppy, myrrh, and lodestone are all Saturnian. For a twenty-first century cruelty-free version of a suffumigation, you could try this:

My Recipe for Banishing Incense

An incense to rid yourself of those nasty habits, behaviours or addictions that are holding you back. To burn an incense, you will need a censor – a heatproof container (either a metal thurible, or an old mug or earthenware dish). Fill it to 1 cm below the top with earth, salt, or sand. You will also need some small charcoal discs – the type used in shisha pipes, so you will find these in a local international supermarket, or online. It is also useful to have a pestle and mortar for this, to grind the ingredients together.

You will need:

2 teaspoons of Frankincense resin
1 teaspoon of Pine Resin (which is Martian, but will give you an extra kick of energy)
1 teaspoon of patchouli herb
Nine drops (3x3) of Cyprus essential oil

On a Saturday, or at the hour of Saturn, begin by grinding the dried herb in a pestle and mortar, then add the resin, and finally the essential oils. As you mix, think about becoming free of the thing you are banishing. You can even read aloud the Orphic Hymn to Saturn as you mix, and when you feel the energy within you reach a pinnacle, say the words, 'And so it is'.

Saturnian Deities

It's probably no surprise that our Saturnian deities are the ones who are associated with death, the afterlife, and liminal spaces – gateways from one place (or state) to another. However, there is another side to these deities. They might be deities of death, but they are also gods of resurrection and life as well.

Osiris

Osiris is the god of death, resurrection, and fertility, and he is also the ruler of fertility, vegetation, and agriculture. While he is Ancient Egyptian in origin, he is still highly influential in the Western Mystery Traditions today. He is known for his distinctive green skin, pharaoh's beard and crown, and his symbolic crook and flail, which he carries across his chest (in what is known as the Osiride position). These represent love and pain, which life cannot be lived without.

Osiris is the consort of Isis, who was murdered by his brother Set in a jealous rage, and his body desecrated, cut into pieces, and scattered to the corners of the earth. Isis then had to go in search of the parts, and using her magic, bring him back to life. On his resurrection he was made the judge of the dead and the underworld, and the god who granted all life. Temple depictions show the souls of the dead kneeling before Osiris, who is often flanked by Isis and their sister Nephthys, as he passes judgement.

He is also associated with the constellation which we now know as Orion.

Hel

In the Norse Pantheon, Hel is one of the children of the trickster god, Loki. Her name means 'Hidden', and like Hades in Greece, her name is also used to refer to the underworld where she presides over the souls of the dead who did not die in battle. There is some debate in academic circles as to whether she is a deity or just a personification of death, but there is a distinct lack of evidence on either side (and female deities are often denied in patriarchal circles!)

Hel can be a challenging (yet rewarding) deity to work with, and her offerings can include pain, difficulty, and toil, not just the usual crystals and foods that most deities are offered. She can represent an arduous task that will take all you have to offer but will benefit generations to come.

Persephone

According to the Homeric hymn, Demeter's daughter Persephone was given the task of painting all the flowers of the earth, but before she could complete this task, she was kidnapped by Hades, the god of the underworld. He took her to his underworld kingdom (named after himself). Distraught at the loss of her daughter, Demeter (the Goddess of Nature) went in search of her daughter and looked high and low for her. To coerce Zeus to allow the return of her daughter, she caused a terrible drought in which the people starved, which meant that the gods were also deprived of sacrifice, one of their favoured forms of worship. Zeus stepped in and Persephone was allowed to return to her mother, however, it was a rule of the Fates that whoever consumed food or drink in the Underworld was doomed to spend eternity there. Before Persephone was released to Hermes, who had been sent to retrieve her, Hades tricked her into eating six pomegranate seeds, which meant Persephone had to return to Hades for six months in every year.

Binah

Binah is the feminine principle associated with Saturn in Kabbalah. She embodies spiritual discernment, stability, awareness, and comprehension. Her name translates at 'the understanding'. Bees are sacred to Binah, as are lilies, and lead. She is associated with the ocean ('I am the soundless, boundless bitter sea' by Dion Fortune), primordial wisdom, and crone energy. Like Saturn, her colour is black, and she is a disciplined teacher who requires discipline, and her virtue is silence, which allows her followers to hear and be open to learning.

Saturnian Tarot

The Death Card

In Modern astrology it is often linked to Pluto, but I always see it as the essence of Saturn.

Most people blanch at the sight of the Death card, but for me it is one of my favourites. The Death card joins us to the spirit of nature, the force many of us have become separated from. There is something about embracing the darkness of Saturn and its dark, muchly, earthy energy that can be very freeing. The Death card can symbolise an actual death, but more frequently it represents the necessary death of something (an idea, a period of your life, a lifestyle, a job etc) and the beginning of a completely new era. Like our Saturnian deities like Osiris, the Death card represents death and the continuation of life. 'Life is immortal, but the living must die,' as the saying goes.

The Death card is the thirteenth of the major arcana, a number which is often viewed with suspicion, and this only adds to the reputation of the card. It comes to remind us that death will claim everyone, king and commoner alike, and like life, it is always present. In our modern worldview of the world and our illusion that we have control over life, we often forget that death is a presence we have no control over. In some religions, people are taught to place their faith in the hope of an afterlife, which Carl Jung has written developed as a way of coping with the idea of death – without the promise of an afterlife, death can seem too monstrous to accept. As anyone who has experienced a major bereavement will tell you, we don't have control over life and death, and when it comes, it sweeps away all logic, all illusions, and only the love remains. Death's ultimate lesson is that if we can accept death, we can live more fully. Death stimulates growth.

The World

On a slightly more optimistic bent, the World card also falls under the dominion of Saturn. This card expresses an understanding, a freedom, and rapture that goes beyond words. The unconscious is now known consciously, and the outer self is unified with the forces of life. This is the ecstatic dance of being. We may reduce these wonders to the ordinary situations we face in life, with which we concern ourselves when we seek out most tarot readings, but the card expresses success, achievements, satisfaction, and a unification of the inner self with outer activities. There is also an element of control implied in this card, in keeping with its planetary ruler.

Practical Saturnian Magic

Saturnian magic holds the qualities of grounding, centring, protecting, banishing, temperance, and stability. This means that if you are in a position of finding your life a little too Mercurial for comfort, Saturn spells can slow things down and give you some slow-moving stability. If you want to end an addiction of any kind or create a more stable home-life for yourself, then you can call on Saturn. You can also combine its energy with that of other planets. For example, combine Saturn with Venus for a stable, long-lasting love.

Grounding Bath Salts

A recipe for a purifying, and grounding sacred bath: Salt is a deep cleanser on an energetic level, and Epsom salts are an old cure for aching muscles.

On a Saturday (or at the hour of Saturn) take one cup of sea salt and half a cup of Epsom salts. Mix them together, whilst picturing your grounding intent. Then add three drops each of patchouli and vetivert essential oils. Then add in three teaspoons of patchouli herb.

Mix well, add a cup full to a nice warm bath, and sit back and soak.

A Saturnian Candle Spell for Grounding

You will need:

A black candle (a 'spell candle' will burn for an hour or two, a dinner sized candle will last a full seven hours, so you might like to invest in some spell candles of mixed colours. I keep a selection of all seven colours in the house, so I have always got one to hand).

A cocktail stick, a pencil or something pointy for carving the candle

Three drops of Patchouli or Cypress essential oil

On a Saturday, take your candle, and carve the Saturnian glyph and your initials onto the candle, and then anoint it with three drops of your essential oil, all the while stating your intended outcome in the present tense (for example, 'it is January 20th and I am safe, confident, and in control of the situation.' Better still, visualise yourself doing something you associate with grounding – spending relaxed time in nature, or even cooking yourself a healthy meal at home in your own kitchen. However small it might seem, it doesn't matter. Really focus on how it feels to be doing that thing. If you struggle with visualisation, try to imagine on what you will see, hear, taste, smell and feel when you get the result. When you have that vision really clear in your mind's eye, or that feeling in your body, visualise all of that going into the candle, then light it, and end with a 'And so it is'.

A Saturn Herb Sachet for Stability

You will need:

A black pouch
A piece of paper or parchment inscribed with your initials and the Saturn Seal (see the Agrippa section) in black ink
Three drops of Patchouli or Cypress essential oil
3 teaspoons of patchouli herb
Three small black crystal tumble stones – obsidian or onyx or jet would be best

On a Saturday, take your pouch and parchment, and draw the Saturnian glyph and your initials onto the paper, and then anoint it with three drops of your essential oil, all the while stating your intended outcome in the present tense. Better still, visualise yourself doing something you associate with stability – spending time at home in your space, or whatever it is you associate with stability. Fold the parchment three times, and place it in the black sachet or pouch, along with three teaspoons of patchouli herb, and the three crystals. Get yourself into the yogic child's pose – kneeling, with your arms outstretched in front of you, with your palms up, and your forehead on the ground. Place the sachet in your upturned palms. Focus on your breath, counting deep breaths in threes, allowing your body to slow down, and become calm. Focus on the feelings of anxiety leaving from your forehead or third eye and draining into the ground. deep breaths. When you have reached a moment of peacefulness, focus your thoughts on that sachet, close your palms around it, and say, 'So Mote it Be'. When you feel the need to tap into those feelings of stability and peacefulness, return to the sachet. You can also place it beneath your pillow at night to allow it to imbue you with its energies while you sleep.

Concluding Thoughts, or 'In This Life We All Die Beginners'

When do we become experts?

I was once asked by a student when they might be considered an expert in Planetary magic, and I found myself reverting to the snippet of wisdom my own teacher gave me in the early years of my study – 'in this life we all die beginners'. Why do I mention this now? Because I have learned through my two decades of working with planetary powers that they can always surprise you. Each time I work a rite or a spell, I learn a nuance I had not considered before, and after two decades of practice, I don't consider myself an expert. This means you may have read this book as a complete beginner and thought of a million other questions that I haven't answered. Or you may have read this book as a fellow-planetary traveller and disagreed with me in a million places. That's fine. No-one can write the perfect book because we are all human. Instead, I offer you this as a starting place for other conversations and explorations.

I do, however, have a few other snippets to share with you.

Familiarity is Key

Getting to know the planets is a process that you should take your time with. Don't expect to learn it all overnight and do settle in for the long-haul. It can be really satisfying, and there is a plethora of ways you can apply planetary magic. In my own practices, everything I do is planetary in essence. My jewellery making, traditional soap making, incense making. Heck, I even have a planetary themed underwear drawer. It means that if I need a hint of Mars about my day, then it's a red undies day, and nobody I encounter is ever any the wiser.

I found that the best way to really start to get familiar with the planets was the same way I was taught (in both my tarot classes and my coven-training) through immersion. I submerged myself in each planet for a period and kept a magical diary during that period as a way of reflecting on what the planet was teaching me. I wore its colours, ate its foods, kept its altar, read its poetry, and worked its magic.

Why Intuitive Systems of Magic Don't Always Work

As we are working magic with our own Unconscious, you could argue that if the correspondences mean something to you, it doesn't really matter what the 'rules' say. However, there is a reason that magical practitioners turn to ancient source texts for guidance – because this works, and it has done for centuries. While I might like the romantic notion of working intuitively, it gives you no frame of reference, and will probably lead to more failed attempts and botched results. Its fine to resent being told what to do, but rejecting the rules is far more effective when you have learned them first.

There is an idea in Hawaiian Huna, that if you practice as part of a tradition, that as you speak the words of that lineage, all the practitioners that came before you line up behind you and add their power to yours. I like to think that is how my own tradition works. As I make magic using the traditional correspondences of the Grimoires, all those magical practitioners who were experts in this field long before I even existed add their essence to mine. So, I would invite you to explore and study a little before you decide to reject these systems of working. In the future, you might decide to go your own way, but you will do so knowing what the ancient systems describe, which is far more powerful than attempting to ride roughshod over something you don't really understand or haven't really worked with.

Combining your planets

I am often asked by students if you must work with each planet in turn, or if you can combine them. While you are learning, it is useful to keep them singular while you get to know their nuances. This will help you to understand how to blend them later. Blending planetary magic is a bit like creating a perfume – to produce something harmonious, you need to know what the base notes, middle notes and high notes need to be, or you could create something that isn't harmonious.

I do work with multiple planets depending on my need. This helps to counteract some of those downsides they can have a tendency towards. For example, if you want a quick windfall, but one that will stick around, then combine Mercury and Jupiter. If you want a long-lasting love that brings passion with it, combine Venus, Mars and Saturn.

There are also times when I have worked with all seven, if the spell is for an outcome that really matters. At this point, I would consider a seven-night spell, where each night I call upon the powers of the appropriate planet of the day to bring about my aim. That has proved to be particularly effective, especially as workings done over a period of several days / weeks / months are often more effective than the big-bang workings you might carry out in a single night.

The important thing is to get in there and start practicing, as that is the best way to learn. So, I would urge you to put the book down, go and get your herb jars out, and start creating magic with the planets. Before you know it, these transformative energies will seep into everything you do and start colouring your world with their magic.

Works Cited

1. Crowley, Aleister (1980) *Book 4* San Francisco: Weiser Books, p. 99.
2. Cunningham, Scott (1983) *Earth Power: Techniques of Natural Magic,* Woodbury, Llewellyn.
3. D'Este, Sorita and Rankine, David (2007) *Practical Planetary Magick: Working the Magick of the Classical Planets in the Western Esoteric Tradition,* London, Avalonia, p. 12.
4. Reid, Ellen Cannon (1997) *The Witches Qabala: The Pagan Path and the Tree of Life,* Boston, Weiser Books, p. 3.
5. Taylor, Thomas (trans. 1792) 'Orphic Hymn to The Moon' *The Hymns of Orpheus* [online]. Available at https://www.sacred-texts.com/cla/hoo/index.htm (Accessed 28th February 2022)
6. Webb, Henry Bertram Law (1911) *Silences of the Moon,* London, Bodley Head, p. 9.
7. Valiente, Doreen (2014) *The Charge of the Goddess,* Milton Keynes, Doreen Valiente Foundation, pp. 12-13.
8. Agrippa, Cornelius (2018) *The Three Books of Occult Philosophy,* Woodbury, Llewellyn pp. 132-133.
9. Taylor, Thomas (trans. 1792) 'Orphic Hymn to Mercury' *The Hymns of Orpheus* [online]. Available at https://www.sacred-texts.com/cla/hoo/index.htm (Accessed 28th February 2022)
10. Taylor, Thomas (trans. 1792) 'Orphic Hymn to Venus' *The Hymns of Orpheus* [online]. Available at https://www.sacred-texts.com/cla/hoo/index.htm (Accessed 28th February 2022)
11. Taylor, Thomas (trans. 1792) 'Orphic Hymn to The Sun' *The Hymns of Orpheus* [online]. Available at https://www.sacred-texts.com/cla/hoo/index.htm (Accessed 28th February 2022)
12. Shakespeare, William (1924) 'Sonnet XXIII', *The Complete Works of William Shakespeare,* London, Clarendon Press, p. 1203.
13. Taylor, Thomas (trans. 1792) 'Orphic Hymn to Mars' *The*

Hymns of Orpheus [online]. Available at https://www.sacred-texts.com/cla/hoo/index.htm (Accessed 28th February 2022)

14. Taylor, Thomas (trans. 1792) 'Orphic Hymn to Jupiter' *The Hymns of Orpheus* [online]. Available at https://www.sacred-texts.com/cla/hoo/index.htm (Accessed 28th February 2022)

15. Taylor, Thomas (trans. 1792) 'Orphic Hymn to Saturn' *The Hymns of Orpheus* [online]. Available at https://www.sacred-texts.com/cla/hoo/index.htm (Accessed 28th February 2022)

Appendix - Planetary Correspondences

Moon Correspondences

Animals	Dogs, crab, turtle, moths, Sphinx, goat, cat
Archangel	Gabriel
Astrology	Cancer
Chakra	Third eye
Colours	White, blue, silver, violet
Crystals	Moonstone, Pearl, Mother of Pearl, Selenite
Day	Monday (Lundi)
Deities	Selene, Diana, Artemis, Hathor, Hekate, Kali, Hera, Aradia
Element	Water and Earth
Foods	Watercress, almond, banana, cucumber, lettuce, fungi, lemon
Herbs	poppy, evening primrose, mallow, iris, mandrake, dittany, mugwort, jasmine, sandalwood, lemon balm
Magic	Women's mysteries, fertility, clairvoyance, divination, cyclical events, dreaming, hereditary qualities
Metals	Silver
Number	9, 81, 369, 3321. Also 28 or 3
Places	Wilderness, woods, rivers, seas, seashores, ships, corn granaries
Qualities	Sedative, soporific, things that live or grow near water, reproductive cycles
Sabbat	Imbolc
Sephiroth	Yesod
Tarot card	The Moon

Mercurial Correspondences

Animals	Dogs, foxes, weasels, hare, civet, 'those that are of both sex and change sex' (Agrippa).	Archangel	Raphael	Astrology	Gemini, Virgo
Chakra	Throat	Colours	Orange	Crystals	Agate, adventuring, mottled jasper, mica
Day	Wednesday (Mercredi)	Deities	Papa Legba, Elegba, Janus, Ganesh, Hermes, Hermaphrodite, Loki, Lugh	Element	Air and water
Foods	Carraway, celery, lemongrass, mint, parsley, pistachio, peels – citrus peel, mace.	Herbs	Lavender, bergamot, dill, fennel, lemon herbs, mint, papyrus, parsley.	Magic	Intellect, study, swiftness, communication, learning, travel, pickpocketing, the stock market
Metals	Mercury (Quicksilver)	Number	8, 64, 260, 2080.	Places	Shops, schools, warehouses, marketplaces, banks.
Qualities	Changeable, trickster, quick, ingenious, a flash of inspiration, or ideas that leave as quickly as they arrived.				
Sabbat	Spring Equinox	Sephiroth	Hod	Tarot card	The Magician

Venusian Correspondences

Animals	Agrippa tells us it is animals who are "Luxurious of strong love – dog, stinky sheep, goat, bull, calf, swan, pigeon, sparrow, swallow, turtle dove".
Archangel	Haniel
Astrology	Taurus and Libra
Chakra	Heart (Anahita)
Colours	Pink (modern), green (traditional).
Crystals	Blue, green and pink calcite, Rose Quartz, chrysocolla, emerald, green jasper, malachite, tourmaline.
Day	Friday (Vendredi)
Deities	Ishtar, Venus, Aphrodite, Inanna, Erzuli Freda, Oshun, Isis, Mary.
Element	Earth
Foods	Coriander, apple, fig, apricot, avocado, pomegranate - Sweet, unctuous, delectable tastes.
Herbs	Rose, hibiscus, geranium, iris, heather, larkspur, lilac, magnolia, willow, mallow, mint, myrtle, violet, maidenhair, ambergris.
Magic	Love and art, physical attraction, sense of harmony and beauty, maiden, sweetheart or mistress.
Metals	Copper (Verdigris)
Number	7, 49, 175, 1225
Places	Cyprus specifically, but also pleasant fountains, green meadows, flourishing gardens, baths, dancing places, women's spaces.
Qualities	Romance, sensuality, self-care, nail painting reconciliation, beauty, youth, joy, happiness, friendship.
Sabbat	Beltane
Sephiroth	Netzach
Tarot card	The Empress

Solar Correspondences

Animals	Archangel	Astrology	Chakra	Colours	Crystals
Agrippa – 'animals of courage, ambitious, renown' - Lion, phoenix, hawk, crocodile.	Michael Raphael	Leo	Solar Plexus	Gold, yellow	Gold, fool's gold, amber, orange calcite, quartz, tiger's eye.

Day	Deities	Element	Foods	Herbs	Magic
Sunday	The sacrificial God – Jesus, Dionysus, Osiris, Ra.	Fire	Olive, saffron, rosemary, chamomile, juniper (gin!) bay, oak, oranges, cloves.	Marigold, bay, saffron, benzoin, cedar, frankincense, sandalwood	Health, healing, protection, success, physical energy, fulfilment.

Metals	Number	Places	Qualities
Gold	6, 36, 111, 666	Sicily, Italy, palaces, theatres.	Sovereignty 'Pure blood and the Spirit of Life – the Solar plexus, the will, authority, it's vice is false pride.

Sabbat	Sephiroth	Tarot card
Yule, Midsummer	Tifareth	The Sun, Strength

Martian Correspondences

Animals	Ram, woodpecker, wolf, bear, serpent, dragon, scorpion.
Archangel	Khamiel
Astrology	Aries, Scorpio
Chakra	Solar plexus, or root
Colours	Red
Crystals	Bloodstone, jasper, flint, garnet, rhodonite, red tourmaline, watermelon tourmaline.
Day	Tuesday (Mardi)
Deities	Ares, Ogun, Chango, Sekhmet, Bellona.
Element	Fire (hot and dry)
Foods	Chilli, basil, coriander, cumin, garlic, ginger, onions, peppers, allspice, basil.
Herbs	Gorse, thistles, tobacco, wormwood, nettle, hawthorn, dragon's blood, broom, cactus.
Magic	Sex, war, courage, aggression, physical strength, healing after surgery, politics, male energy, defensiveness.
Metals	Iron and brass.
Number	5, 25, 65, 325
Places	Fiery, hot places, volcanos, execution places, battlegrounds.
Qualities	Energy and action, courage and determination, impulsiveness, ruthlessness.
Sabbat	Lammas
Sephiroth	Geburah (Might)
Tarot card	The Emperor, the Tower

Jupiterian Correspondences

Animals	Eagle, elephant, swallow, stork, dolphin.
Archangel	Tzadiel
Astrology	Pisces, Sagittarius
Chakra	Sacral
Colours	Purple, royal blue
Crystals	Amethyst, lepidolite, sugilite.
Day	Thursday
Deities	Zeus, Thor, Papa Legba.
Element	Air
Foods	Sweet and pleasant tastes - clove, mace, pheasant
Herbs	basil, mace, violet, oak, barley, wheat, borage, star anise, honeysuckle, betony, dock, horse chestnut.
Magic	Harmony, law, religion, expansion and enlargement, ownership, wealth and fortune, music, benevolent rulership
Metals	Silver and Gold
Number	4, 16, 34, 136
Places	Privileged places, noble places, beautiful and clean spaces with diverse odours.
Qualities	Harmony, expansion and enlargement, ownership, benevolent rulership
Sabbat	Autumn Equinox
Sephiroth	Chesed
Tarot card	Wheel of Fortune

Saturnian Correspondences

Animals	Creeping, slow, solitary, contemplative. Bear, mole, cat, camel, toad, serpent, bat, crow, owl.
Archangel	Tzafkiel
Astrology	Capricorn and Aquarius
Chakra	Root
Colours	Black and brown.
Crystals	Onyx, brown jasper, lodestone, Apache tear, coal, haematite, obsidian, jet, black tourmaline.
Magic	Grounding, centring, protection, banishing, security, certainty, temperance, stability, agriculture, old age.
Herbs	Amaranth, beech, mandrake, opium, belladonna, comfrey, elm, hemlock, henbane, ivy, tamarind, tamarisk, wolfsbane, yew, patchouli, vetivert, oak moss.
Foods	Sour, tart, dead. Beetroot, potato, root vegetables, tamarind.
Qualities	Slow moving, loss and grieving, endings, stability, grounding.
Places	Graveyards, tombs, empty houses, stinking, dark, underground, caves, still pools.
Element	Earth
Deities	Baron Samedi, Osiris, Papa Legba, The Morrigan, Hel, Shani
Number	3, 9, 15, 45.
Metals	Lead and gold
Day	Saturday
Tarot card	Death
Sephiroth	Binah
Sabbat	Samhain

Further Reading

I would encourage you to track these titles down in your local library or independent bookshop.

Agrippa, Cornelius, *The Three Books of Occult Philosophy.*

Anon, *The Lesser Key of Solomon.*

Bandler, Richard & Grinder, John, *The Structure of Magic: A Book About Language and Therapy.*

Barrett, Francis, *The Magus.*

Cannon Reid, Ellen, *The Witches Qabala: The Pagan Path and the Tree of Life.*

Crowley, Aleister, *Book 4.*

Culpepper, Nicholas, *Complete Herbal.*

Cunningham, Scott, *Earth Power: Techniques of Natural Magic.*

Cunningham, Scott, *The Complete Book of Incense, Oils, and Brews.*

D'Este, Sorita and Rankine, David, *Practical Planetary Magick: Working the Magick of the Classical Planets in the Western Esoteric Tradition.*

Davies, Owen, *Cunning Folk: Popular Magic in English History.*

Dunn, Patrick (trans.) *The Orphic Hymns.*

Hardy, Robert, *The Witches' Hexagram: A Wiccan View of the Cabbala.*

Hutton, Ronald, *The Triumph of the Moon: A History of Modern Pagan Witchcraft.*

Jung, Carl, *The Archetypes, and the Collective Unconscious.*

Kelly, Edmund (trans.) *The Picatrix.*

Taylor, Thomas (trans.) *The Hymns of Orpheus.*

Valiente, Doreen, *The Charge of the Goddess.*

Webb, Henry Bertram Law, *Silences of the Moon.*

If you have enjoyed this book and would like to find out more, or for more information about my writing and research, you can find me at www.rebeccabeattie.co.uk.

Feedback is always a wonderful thing, positive or otherwise. Please do get in touch, as I would love to hear from you. Also, reviews on your favourite online sites such as Amazon are always important to a writer, as they can really help other people make the decision to read your work and will encourage the writer to keep writing! If you have enjoyed this book and would like to help others find it, please do leave reviews on Amazon or on Goodreads or anywhere else you feel able to.

**MOON
BOOKS**

PAGANISM & SHAMANISM

What is Paganism? A religion, a spirituality, an alternative belief system, nature worship? You can find support for all these definitions (and many more) in dictionaries, encyclopaedias, and text books of religion, but subscribe to any one and the truth will evade you. Above all Paganism is a creative pursuit, an encounter with reality, an exploration of meaning and an expression of the soul. Druids, Heathens, Wiccans and others, all contribute their insights and literary riches to the Pagan tradition. Moon Books invites you to begin or to deepen your own encounter, right here, right now.

If you have enjoyed this book, why not tell other readers by posting a review on your preferred book site.

Recent bestsellers from Moon Books are:

Journey to the Dark Goddess
How to Return to Your Soul
Jane Meredith
Discover the powerful secrets of the Dark Goddess and
transform your depression, grief and pain into healing
and integration.
Paperback: 978-1-84694-677-6 ebook: 978-1-78099-223-5

Shamanic Reiki
Expanded Ways of Working with Universal Life Force Energy
Llyn Roberts, Robert Levy
Shamanism and Reiki are each powerful ways of healing; together,
their power multiplies. *Shamanic Reiki* introduces techniques to
help healers and Reiki practitioners tap ancient healing wisdom.
Paperback: 978-1-84694-037-8 ebook: 978-1-84694-650-9

Pagan Portals – The Awen Alone
Walking the Path of the Solitary Druid
Joanna van der Hoeven
An introductory guide for the solitary Druid, *The Awen Alone* will
accompany you as you explore, and seek out your own place
within the natural world.
Paperback: 978-1-78279-547-6 ebook: 978-1-78279-546-9

A Kitchen Witch's World of Magical Herbs & Plants
Rachel Patterson
A journey into the magical world of herbs and plants, filled with
magical uses, folklore, history and practical magic. By popular
writer, blogger and kitchen witch, Tansy Firedragon.
Paperback: 978-1-78279-621-3 ebook: 978-1-78279-620-6

Naming the Goddess
Trevor Greenfield
Naming the Goddess is written by over eighty adherents and
scholars of Goddess and Goddess Spirituality.
Paperback: 978-1-78279-476-9 ebook: 978-1-78279-475-2

Shapeshifting into Higher Consciousness
Heal and Transform Yourself and Our World with Ancient
Shamanic and Modern Methods
Llyn Roberts
Ancient and modern methods that you can use every day to
transform yourself and make a positive difference in the world.
Paperback: 978-1-84694-843-5 ebook: 978-1-84694-844-2

Readers of ebooks can buy or view any of these bestsellers by
clicking on the live link in the title. Most titles are published in
paperback and as an ebook. Paperbacks are available in traditional
bookshops. Both print and ebook formats are available online.

Find more titles and sign up to our readers' newsletter at
http://www.johnhuntpublishing.com/paganism
Follow us on Facebook at https://www.facebook.com/MoonBooks
and Twitter at https://twitter.com/MoonBooksJHP